D1622179

YOU CAN'T DO EVERYTHING . . .
SO DO SOMETHING

You Can't Do Everything . . . So Do Something

Small Ways to Change the World

Shane Stanford

Abingdon Press
Nashville

YOU CAN'T DO EVERYTHING . . . SO DO SOMETHING
SMALL WAYS TO CHANGE THE WORLD

This book is printed on acid-free paper.

Library of Congress Cataloging-in-Publication Data

Stanford, Shane, 1970–
    You can't do everything—so do something : small ways to change the world / Shane Stanford.
        p. cm.
    ISBN 978-1-4267-0590-8 (pbk.: alk. paper)
    1. Christian life.   2. Service (Theology)   I. Title.
BV4520.S665   2010
248.4—dc22

                                                                                        2009052281

10 11 12 13 14 15 16 17 18 19—10 9 8 7 6 5 4 3 2

MANUFACTURED IN THE UNITED STATES OF AMERICA

For the unknown,
unspoken heroes
whose "SOMEthings" mean
EVERYthing to so many

ev•ery•thing
[**ev**-re-thing]—every thing or particular of an aggre-
gate or total; all

some•thing
[**suhm**-thing]—a person or thing of some value or
consequence

an•y•thing
[**en**-ee-thing]—any thing whatever; something, no
matter what

Contents

Contents

Above the Timberline,
Below the Waterline

The best music comes out of wood grown in two places: above the timberline, and below the waterline.

Above the timberline is where the trees have to fight for their very existence. Rapper Talib Kweli, in his hit song "Love Language" (2000), sings how "you know a flower that grow in the ghetto / know more about survival than the one from fresh meadows." Growth that has to fight to grow understands the source of its growth, and the love it gives back to that source makes it extremely dense and resonant. The maple wood chosen by Antonio Stradivari (1644–1737) to craft many of the violins we've branded "Stradivarius" came from the forests of northern Croatia, where the harsh winters create a slow-growth "Croatian wood" prized by luthiers to this day.

Below the waterline is the source for the best woods for electric guitars. "Swamp ash" is the portion of the ash tree that grows below the waterline in swamps and bayous of the Deep South. It is light, resonant, and the preferred "vintage wood" on Fender Stratocasters, Telecasters, and similar guitars. To harvest this wood you need to fight off the gators and snakes.

In *You Can't Do Everything . . . So Do Something*, Shane Stanford shows how the best instruments of God's grace and love come from slow and steady growth, often under adverse conditions, and that don't attempt to reach maturity too quickly. When I first read Shane's title, I thought of all those years when I was a pastor. Whenever anyone in my church said, "Why doesn't the church do something?" I heard them really saying, "Why don't YOU do something?" In a world where to do "nothing" is not an option, this book issues a call for all to do something, whether you're a tortoise among hares or a hare among tortoises. Besides, in Japanese fables, tortoises *do* win races.

My greatest discovery in reading this book was the realization that when we keep on keeping on, when we keep playing and playing, even when we don't feel like playing or wonder whether anyone is listening, our wood actually ages along with our playing and makes the quality of the tonal sound even greater. If you don't believe me, go to one of Willie Nelson's 200 gigs a year, where he brings out the most beautiful guitar on the planet, "Trigger," which Nelson has used since 1969. Trigger is weathered, sweat-stained, beaten up, written on, as one might expect after 300 albums, 2,000 songs, and 40-plus years of playing. But this guitar has major mojo and produces one of the most distinctive, resonant sounds in the world of music today.

Just like this book.

Leonard Sweet
Drew University, George Fox University, sermons.com

Acknowledgments

With as much as I have written within these pages, no book could hold everything I would want to say to those who have meant so much to me along the journey. Thus, to everyone who has guided me with thoughts and prayers, I offer a heartfelt thank you. Your name may not be listed here, but I hope you know who you are and how much you mean to me.

The following is an attempt to thank those individuals who remain at the center of everything I am and all that I do. They are the cheering squad and my balance when life gets out of control. If it weren't for these folks, none of this would be possible.

To everyone at Abingdon Press, for making this process much easier than it should have been.

To Chip MacGregor, a wonderful agent and friend, for being convinced that what I have to say truly means something.

To dear friends and marvelous people who inform and challenge me every day.

To my friends and colleagues in ministry, for your support and patience.

To my family—Mom, Buford, Whitney, Dad, Patty, Nanny, Delana, Tracy, Randy, Kimberly, and Memaw—for, once more, believing in me more than I believe in myself.

To Sarai Grace, Juli Anna, and Emma Leigh, for being EVERYthing, SOMEthing, and ANYthing all rolled into one. I love you.

To my wife, Pokey. You are my treasure. I love you.

To Jesus, my dearest friend, for doing everything I couldn't and for giving me something so incredibly undeserved. Your grace is sufficient.

INTRODUCTION
"Just One Other Thing . . ."

Mark 10:17-24

People loved asking Jesus questions. Why wouldn't they? He was open, approachable, respected. His demeanor provided acceptance to just about everyone who came to him, whether it was a Pharisee or a common person from the dusty streets. Jesus loved people—and he loved talking to them about their ideas, conditions, and solutions. Yes, it was easy to ask questions of Jesus.

But people did not necessarily like Jesus' answers. They were a different bag. Though Jesus encouraged openness and acceptance, he also spoke the truth, was honest in his replies, and provided, sometimes to his own detriment, the most straightforward of responses, even on the most delicate of topics.

Some who came to Jesus walked away with a sense of justification and strength. Others strolled away burdened by the thought of how far they were from being able to live what he had just offered and encouraged. All left very different than before.

The real gifts of Jesus' responses were that he spoke about real significance and answers in a world that so often asks meaningless questions. Jesus would never settle for telling you what you wanted to hear, but he would most certainly share with you what you needed. The gap between these two offered times of great joy and affirmation, but also great anxiety and disappointment. Sure, as Jesus said, the "truth will make you free" (see John 8:32); but many times freedom has a price.

Take one rich, young man's encounter with Jesus for instance. . . .

In the familiar account of the rich, young ruler (Mark 10), Jesus encounters a young man who believes he has all the rules of life in order. According to the standards of the young man's world, he probably did. We assume by Mark's description that he was a good man, with position, title, and also enough spiritual maturity that he comes to Jesus to ask what to him is an important question: "Teacher, what must I do to inherit eternal life?" (v. 17). We have all asked such questions, and in such ways as to get the answer we want, but not necessarily the one we need.

Jesus gave the latter. Jesus sensed that the young man was a good, noble person; so he said, "Keep the commandments." To which the young man replied, "I have done just that." The young man seemed proud of his reply and happy that he was headed down the right path. Who wouldn't be? He had just given the right answer to the right man. I am sure the young man stopped to look around, maybe even to peer at his neighbors and colleagues to make sure they heard his interchange with Jesus. All seemed right.

Then, at the end of their discussion, just as the young man was about to turn and leave, Jesus asked "one other thing." Oh, how I hate the "one other thing." When I was younger and got into trouble, I could usually talk myself out of most jams. But my mother, who was wise to my verbal acrobatics and keen debating skills (or, at least, the ones I had built up in my mind), would always give me enough room to feel, at least, that I was about to win the conversation—until the "one other thing." This "one other thing" would have to do with the piece of information I had left out of the story or the words left unsaid or the intention that I had not fully disclosed. No matter what or who or where the "one other thing" was, it was the very thing that was usually my downfall.

Of course, we know the end of the story and the effect Jesus' "one other thing" had on this young man. Jesus said to him, in effect, "Okay, then, you have kept the commandments. One other thing: go and sell all you have, and give it to the poor." "What did he just say?" one of the bystanders must have whispered. I am sure the rich, young ruler was thinking it as well. Sell . . . give . . . poor? But . . . We know how the story ends. The Scripture says the young man turned away "sad," because . . . *one other thing* . . . he was very rich. The young man wanted more; he wanted significance. But significance requires "one other thing." It always has a price.

Caller ID

The first time I saw the caller ID that day, I ignored it. It read *Saddleback Community Church*. I had known of Saddleback Community Church in Lake Forest, California, of Rick and Kay Warren and their Purpose Driven movement, for nearly ten years. The impact they had made was unquestionable. What had started as any other megachurch experience had, over the last decade, transformed into one of the most significant ministries in the world. And it wasn't just Rick's multimillion selling book *A Purpose Driven Life*. No, the book had opened doors that would allow them to unveil other parts of their hearts, the deeper parts, and God would bless them for it.

Kay's transformation was the driving force behind the new direction in the couple's, as well as the church's, life. Rick had experienced immense success with the book, but it was Kay's fight with breast cancer and her convalescence that led to the real life-changing events of the couple's journey.

While looking at a magazine cover that included a picture of young children dying of AIDS in Africa, Kay became, in her words, seriously disturbed. From here, God pushed her around until she convinced Rick, whose own heart was being changed too, to take note of the incredible challenges the developing world faced in terms of poverty, disease, and community development.

At first, Kay believed God simply wanted her to go to Africa and to see what the condition was for those in such need. God's plan, however, was much larger than one trip. Eventually, Kay, with Rick's blessing, would establish a new initiative at Saddleback for HIV/AIDS awareness and would, almost single-handedly, challenge the prevailing evangelical notions of the disease.

As Kay described it, God would unveil a part of his plan and she would respond, only to have God ask for "one other thing." That "one other thing" eventually expanded their initiative into a worldwide summit that included the likes of Bono, Bill and Melinda Gates, Hillary Rodham Clinton, Franklin Graham, and a senator from Illinois who would be elected President of the United States.

The summit was not the final expression of God's plan for their new work. Eventually the P.E.A.C.E. plan emerged to tackle other global issues including malaria, intense poverty, and malformed educational and cultural systems. The miracle behind the plan was that from that magazine cover came a series of new horizons that, as they unfolded one layer at a time, became more than just programs, conferences, or events; they became a movement and a cultural statement from the evangelical church: God was calling out the church to "do something" . . . no details, action plans, or grand strategies would be needed at first . . . just "something." God would take care of the rest.

Take care of it he has. Thousands of Christians have responded to the call to live as co-belligerents in the fight against pandemic issues meant to destroy our world. This means that folks who usually would never work together because of the vastness of what they do not agree on have decided to cooperate and work together based on the one cause they find common ground in—eradicating the giant issues of our world. Whereas nonprofits and governments have done their part, it has been the church that has transformed the conversation about how the developing world can and will be touched by the resource-rich, predominantly white evangelical church in America. But more important, through this "something," the "one other thing" has unveiled how the global church will ultimately redefine and transform the church in America and around the world.

What I did not know about the caller ID was that it was Kay Warren's office calling to invite me to speak at the 2006 Global AIDS Summit at Saddleback Church. I answered a second phone call and, in December 2006, had the privilege of meeting Rick and Kay and participating in that year's summit. I also had a chance to meet unbelievable people, including then-Senator and future-President Barack Obama. But, as tremendous an honor as it was to meet these exceptional people, it was the other folks who really impressed me: a woman from Ethiopia who ran a day orphanage for children abandoned to HIV. Or the congressional aide using his own vacation time to attend the Summit because of an interview he had seen with Kay Warren. Or a worker for Samaritan's Purse who had given up a lucrative law career after finishing at Harvard Law School because God, as she put it, "would not leave me alone." For three days, I met people who gave and shared and volunteered and sacrificed because they knew of no other way to satisfy this desire for something significant.

I had the privilege that year of speaking in the very first session of the event. On stage, it was Rick, Kay, and I. I remember sitting there thinking how long the journey had been for this HIV-positive pastor from Mississippi who, just a few years earlier, had been turned away from his first church because of his HIV status. Now here I was, sitting on one of the most important stages in America with the person who arguably was (and who most certainly later would become) the most significant pastor in the country.

Rick introduced me, and I gave my testimony. After the first session, the security team whisked us away to a news conference where Rick and Kay spoke to worldwide media outlets about the Summit's purpose. CNN, FOX News, MSNBC, and other media members were there to hear the story, the challenge of how this conference could make a difference. Many of the secular folks were skeptical. The issues being discussed seemed daunting and overwhelming. How was it that this pastor from California believed that he could do anything about what the United Nations was having trouble addressing?

To be quite honest, I had wondered this too. I was excited to be at the Summit and to tell my story, but the objectives were more than ambitious; they seemed almost impossible.

As we prepared to enter the press conference, security stopped us at the door. It would be a few moments before the press conference was to begin. Realizing that I might not have this chance again, standing next to this man and this woman who were doing their part to change the world and who believed so passionately in the ability of the church to do just that, I thought I would take my chance and ask the question. It was the question to which most of the folks at the Summit wanted to know the answer, one that the secularists could not understand, and one that the faithful could not really, deep down, find room to believe. It was a tough question, because it hinted at the magnitude of all we knew was happening and of what was being discussed. We wanted it to be true, and we wanted this gathering and those like it to be real. So, I asked the question anyway.

Looking at Rick, I said, "So, Rick, given all that we have to do and all that we have to overcome, what would you say to the church who, for this moment, decides to believe it can become everything you say God believes we can? What is the best advice for us, beyond our doubts and uncertainties, if we decide to move forward?"

I had heard Rick mention many times the vastness that people feel when they confront these huge issues. The feel from each response was that "You can't do everything . . . but do something." Sure, we would not be able to effect change in every situation or corner of our lives, but we certainly could effect the change that God had gifted in each of us and had put in front of us.

The conference concluded, and my wife, Pokey, and I made our way back to Mississippi, where I was serving a church. I had written Rick's phrase on the back of a napkin at the hotel that same evening and later pinned it to my office wall. It would be weeks before I would think of it again. The morning my devotional came from Mark 10 and the story of the rich, young ruler, I remember looking at the note pinned to my wall.

The challenge for the young man in the story was that he had been led to believe that in order to be significant or to accomplish significant things he needed to do "everything," to be "everything." Nothing could be further from the truth. The real challenge was that in trying to be or do "everything," we often miss the "something" that God had given to us to accomplish. Sure, it was often the deepest, most personal of "somethings" that required of us more than all of the rest of the "somethings" put together; but it was ours. If God had blessed us to make it ours, God most certainly would bless us with the ability to do it and do it well when the time came.

Where do we spend most of our time—"trying to do everything" until the "something" is out of room or out of energy or out of mind? To make matters worse, because so many "somethings" do not get done, then almost "nothing" is achieved for the greatest needs and potential of the church. The results, or the lack thereof, are vivid and often speak for themselves.

Yet, let's think for a moment about the inverse. What if we realize that we can't do everything, and so we decide that we will focus on our particular "something" that God has given us to do, to be, or to accomplish. When everyone is focused on his or her *something*, then anything is possible. Not because we have it all under control, but because God's plan is now working.

Paul talks about this in 1 Corinthians 12, in his discussion of the body of believers. God realizes our limitations, our frail and fragile boundaries as individuals. As the body of Christ, though, when the arms, the eyes, the feet, and the hands are all working together, then there is nothing that can't be accomplished. Yes, I said *nothing*. Rick Warren's advice—"You can't do everything . . . but do something"—was the first part of a much deeper understanding of God and of the whole. Take the example of a tapestry, seen from the back and then from the front. It looks like a mess from the back, with its threads all woven together; but when it all comes into place, and you see it from the front, you are amazed at how all of it fits together.

Remember that Jesus' conversation with the rich, young ruler was not a rebuke at all, quite the opposite. "You have focused on the 'everything' for so long that you have forgotten the 'one thing' that means the most," Jesus seems to offer. "Your wealth and willingness to give it away is not just your 'one other thing,' it is your 'something,' and it will change your life."

Expendable

I am about to give away my age and my generational leanings. Do you remember the movie *Rambo: First Blood Part II*? In case you haven't seen it, consider this a SPOILER alert. In a great scene in the movie Rambo, played by Sylvester Stallone, explains to his Vietnamese guide why he was sent to North Vietnam to find American prisoners of war (POWs), and how then, after finding them, he basically was ignored and left to die. *"Why would your own people do that to you?"* is the young woman's question. In what may very well be the best part of the movie, Rambo explains that he is "expendable," so that whether he does or doesn't find POWs, the government can walk away from him without much regard for what happens. Not only is the mission a farce, but because Rambo is "expendable," the consequences are manageable and don't mean much either. Later, as the young guide is dying after an attack from the enemy, she struggles in her last breath to tell Rambo that she does not think he is "expendable." After she dies, Rambo ties her necklace around his neck and proceeds to wreak havoc upon the enemy and upon those of his own camp who betrayed him in the mission. Now, I realize that Rambo's methods are questionable, and I certainly do not condone the violence or explicit nature of the movie. The point of the illustration, though, is not to get you to watch the movie, but to realize an important point about having someone truly believe you matter—that you have worth and purpose in this world. It is amazing, what one person believing in someone else can mean for the possibilities of what that person can then accomplish. In the very last scene of the movie, the American bureaucrat who betrayed Rambo basically explains that his actions were due to the fact that Rambo wasn't really supposed to matter so much; he wasn't supposed to succeed. But Rambo's friend convinced him that he did matter, and it changed everything.

Though you may never have said it out loud, it is possible you may believe that when it comes to you, the church, and God's plan, you are expendable. After all, most of us will never change our world, at least not the way the world says it likes to be changed. For most of us, our lives and our gifts are not flashy, and we certainly possess neither the means for exacting large-scale projects and summits, nor are we able to march through the proverbial jungle carrying an M-9 around our neck (like Rambo). So, if we can't do something like this, then what can we really contribute? As the conversation goes further, if we really can't contribute or make a significant difference, then why would we sacrifice our own comforts or ambitions for others?

This book is, however, not about sacrifice and service as we have so often been taught. And it is certainly not about expendable people. On the contrary, this book is about the joy of giving back that which was built and created in us to be given back from the beginning. Not only does that make us useful; it also makes us valuable because it is how we are wired up. It is just that in the process of trying to accomplish so many other things in this world, things that the world has defined as important or necessary, we forget about the "one other thing" that was supposed to give us the most joy, the most presence, and the most purpose.

We can't accomplish everything; that seems to be a pretty simple, straightforward truth. Why, then, do so many of us have trouble with it? What is it that the Adversary has done in and around us that convinces us we have to be everything to everyone in order to make a significant contribution in the world?

Kay Warren realized that no matter what she and her husband had accomplished, there was something missing, something personal in God's plan that belonged only to her. When she couldn't identify it within the models of church success that she had known for so many years, the Lord "seriously disturbed" her perspective; and the rest is history.

God does the same thing to you and me. No matter what we have done or have left undone in this world, our purpose and potential still rest in that "something" that God has so beautifully crafted inside of us. It is not meant to confuse or disturb us, though it will if we continue to ignore or downplay its significance. No, more important, the "something" fits within a bigger plan that goes to the heart of our connection in community and in faith and in the future of what God has in store for us all.

This simple book is about finding that "something" in your life and about facing the challenges and obstacles when the need—and, frankly, the expectation—to accomplish everything comes along. Not only will you realize that feeling you have to do everything is not how God intended for his grace to unfold in your life, but hopefully you will discover also how such a philosophy works against the biblical model for how the entire church, the body of Christ, is supposed to work in the first place.

And, yet, finally, this book is also about the possibilities of what happens when we do get it right. There is nothing quite like the body of Christ when it takes hold of what God has planted in each of us. It is profound and personal and poignant. More important, it is perfect, and great things happen because of it.

Giving Hope to Orphans in Africa

Jack spent most of his life as the quintessential United Methodist pastor. Even after God called him to start a new church, he did so with the same fervor and skill that had led him throughout his career. Everyone you talk to, colleagues, friends, family, all love Jack. You instantly see in Jack his humility and his love for God. But you also see an incredible love for God's people, born from a deep spiritual mission that, over the last few years, has changed thousands of lives.

In 2004, Jack's life changed when he was baptized by fire as he confronted face to face the incredible needs in sub-Saharan Africa. These needs haunted Jack. What could he do? He had committed just a few years before to plant a new church. Surely God was not calling him to leave that mission for another new start; it did not make any sense. First, Jack thought of simply organizing trips and teams to go to Africa to help. But God kept calling for more—there was always "one other thing" in Jack's conversations with God.

Finally, to the surprise of his congregation, family, and, most important, to Jack himself, he left the pastoral ministry and founded a new ministry as a means for organizing teams and groups to address the needs of orphans, particularly those in Zimbabwe. Jack found that not only was the need great, but the skills with which God had gifted him came to life in this project. After only a year, over a thousand orphans had found assistance, love, and support through his ministry.

God did not stop there. In the next five years, Jack's ministry expanded to Rwanda, Kenya, and Zambia. Today, there are staff offices in the United States and in Africa. Moving beyond basic-response supplies, the programs now also provide for long-term support and success for persons affected by the HIV / AIDS crisis in Africa, especially the children. Today, children and their families who only a few years ago would have struggled to meet their basic daily needs now have access to training and life opportunities that not only can change their lives but possibly can change their communities as well. All because one man did "something."

The first time I met Jack was at a meeting of the United Methodist Global AIDS Fund. As I sat down at the table, I did not recognize the man sitting across from me. Jack is a humble, incredibly focused, yet seemingly ordinary man. His presence does not particularly overwhelm you—until he begins to share his passion for children and families around the world who are hurting. Jack, in his very ordinary way, has lived out an extraordinary plan for his life.

One of the first times I heard Jack speak, he told of those first days in his former life and of confronting, the first time, those issues of horror and hope in sub-Saharan Africa. Jack said his first intuition was to "do something," but that seemed so insignificant, so inconsequential. Therefore, he began to think in large, grand terms about what could be done. The more he thought about it, the more discouraged he became as he grew overwhelmed by what he had seen and learned about the pandemic and those affected. Forty million AIDS orphans; 14,000 people dying daily from bad water and not enough food; intense discrimination against young girls and women; and incredibly unstable political structures that made almost any plan risky and seemingly undoable. Jack was more than convinced by the need; he was seriously disturbed; and he knew that God wanted him to do something. Yet, what could one person do? Why was God burdening his soul for such an unbelievable, unreachable task?

That is when, Jack said, the Holy Spirit simply intervened, and he heard God speak into his soul. The Holy Spirit, Jack would later tell me, simply encouraged him to follow. Nothing more, nothing less. Jack did follow, creating his ministry, as he puts it, as a means of one small way to respond to the crisis; and the lives of thousands of children have not been the same since.

Jack finished his presentation with these words: "I don't know what God wants from you, but I know he wants something. It was planted like a seed inside of you from the beginning, and he expects and needs for it to grow and blossom. All you are asked to do is water and nurture it—nothing more, nothing less. God will do the rest."

God certainly will.

So here is the real question for you; yes, you. You have picked up this book and have decided to read it. You may even be wondering why—after all, you could have picked up the newest legal thriller or a book by another theologian or a book about marriage or parenting or anything, really. . . . But God led you here, to think about your "something" and about what God needs from you.

So, what will it be? God has already said you can't do everything. In fact, you were never intended to. So, the pressure is off, right? But is it? Because God has also said that each of us has been gifted for something special. You don't have to wonder whether you are a part of the plan; you are! Because of that, you have a valuable part to play, whether you knew it or wanted it before.

The questions are now about you and about what seriously disturbs your life, what keeps you up at night, what bothers your soul so deeply that you wish it would simply be quiet. But it won't be quiet . . . trust me. It wouldn't for the rich, young ruler; it wouldn't for Kay Warren, Jack, or me. It won't for you, either. There is too much at stake, too much to be done. Like it or not, you have been created to be a part of what a living, active God is ALWAYS doing in this world. Sure, God will fill in the blanks and gaps if you decide to walk in another direction. But it won't be the same for any of us—for you, me, and those you were supposed to help—those who, together with you, are meant to change the world.

So, what am I asking? That you devote a few pages to this discussion. There will be places in the course of your reading for you to talk back, to ask questions. There also will be plenty of opportunities for you to disagree. Along the way, I believe you will see God's bigger Word (with a capital "W") calling you, pushing you into something that maybe you have not even imagined possible yet. Yes, you will probably think of all the reasons why you can't go where God is leading. Don't feel bad, everyone does it. Everyone learns that God already anticipates our excuses even before we come up with them. You are simply asked to listen, learn, and, eventually, follow. God will unveil the rest. Maybe by the end, you will be amazed and blessed by the something God has planted in you. That something will be significant.

True significance rests deeper than the world's standards for success. Significance, as defined by God, lies beyond the "one other thing" in each of our lives. However, so many times, we either acquiesce to the world's expectations or become overwhelmed by what seem to be insurmountable odds, and we miss the beauty of what God does in and through us. God understands our frustrations and limitations and offers us a chance to respond to the needs of our world and to make a difference for the Kingdom. It is our personal imprint for Kingdom work. All we need to do is accept it and use it. Success, as the world defines it, can't measure or celebrate God's gift in us. No, we realize success in how God uses us for a plan and for a purpose. Our "one other thing" unveils a spectacular truth in our relationship with God: it is the simple ways and places in which we encounter God that have the most profound impact. Deep down, I believe all of us already know this.

PART I

"You Can't Do EVERYthing . . ."

You Catch the Ball

Ray Perkins probably is best known as the man who followed Paul "Bear" Bryant as the head football coach at the University of Alabama in the early 1980s. It says a lot about a man to be not only willing to follow a legend like Coach Bryant, but also eager for such a challenge. Coach Perkins was and is a person unafraid of a difficult challenge or situation. In fact, he thrives in those situations.

That has been his nature since he played football at the University of Alabama in the mid-1960s on three Crimson Tide teams that won three SEC titles and two National Championships. Ray would later be drafted by the Baltimore Colts and would play in Super Bowl V.

During that time, Ray, who played wide receiver, caught passes from such notable quarterbacks as Joe Namath, Kenny Stabler, and Johnny Unitas, three of the most successful and famous quarterbacks in football history. When you looked at each one, though, the three quarterbacks could not be more different. Namath was flashy and liked the "big play." Stabler was a southpaw and known for quick patterns and precision throws. Unitas, with his legendary arm and tenacious leadership skills, remains one of the most prolific, winning players in history.

I had the privilege of both serving as Ray Perkins's pastor and, later, calling him my dear friend. Growing up, I was more than aware of who he was, of his records as a player, and of his tenures as a college and NFL head coach. Much more important to me, I later had the chance to know the man. Ray's personality can be gruff and, at times, a bit "stand-offish." People sometimes mistake that for aloofness and for arrogance. Nothing could be further from the truth. In fact, during my time as a pastor, I have never met a more caring, giving, sincere person. Certainly Ray lives by a set of strict personal standards that he often holds others to as well. But through my interactions with him, I have found a genuine child of God and a dear friend.

When Ray was inducted into the Mississippi Sports Hall of Fame, a teammate of his told me that Coach Bear Bryant considered Ray one of the most talented all-around athletes he had ever coached, and that was the reason that Coach Bryant believed that Ray's coaching skills, work ethic, and leadership were a perfect combination for following him as coach at Alabama.

The one topic you can get Ray to talk at length about was his playing days at Alabama and then, later, Baltimore in the NFL. To have played with such incredible people and to have been coached by the likes of Bear Bryant and Don Shula (who coached the Baltimore Colts) makes Ray Perkins one of the more intriguing people in football history. His stories prove my assessment. To hear the inside workings of these great, legendary teams is nothing short of amazing.

One of the most memorable conversations we had was when Ray described what it was like to be on teams that included such larger-than-life personalities. Ray told me that it was not like people imagined. Sure, each of those players was great in his own way. But, it wasn't like in the movies. Joe Namath was one of the most exciting players to watch, but he could also throw as many interceptions as touchdowns. Ken Stabler was like a rifle, but he was much quieter than people knew. And Johnny Unitas was one of the greatest quarterbacks to ever play the game, a real legend. But Johnny still had to fight for his job by the time Ray came to the Colts.

Ray said they were different in their own unique ways but also had the same thing in common—when they threw the ball, they needed someone to catch it. Ray would always smile at me when he made this point, and then he would remind me that no quarterback could catch his own pass, unless it is a "broken play."

You can't do everything. If you think you can, well, something is really broken somewhere.

In this section of the book, we address the ways in which we either believe or are convinced that we are responsible for achieving unworkable, unreachable goals in the Christian experience, and then how those feelings often dominate our spiritual walk and dynamics. Quite frankly, our expectations grow to a point that we ultimately build a series of unreasonable goals, objectives, tasks, or expectations that dominate our spiritual journey.

Now I am not saying that we should not reach for big goals. In fact, I am a great supporter of the B.A.G.s of a generation ago. "Big Audacious Goals" have resulted in some of the most remarkable developments in church growth and in the ways the church has responded to the needs of our world. When, however, those goals come to define our processes and expectations to a point that we are unable to achieve the goals, and when we allow them to project our value and focus for the next steps, the results are that we oftentimes become overwhelmed with the task. We burn out; and we miss both the mark of accomplishing the God-given tasks that each of us has been given and also the joy and power of having done these things together.

So over the next few pages, using the first five letters in the word *everything* as an acrostic, I want you to think about the "EVERYthings" that we believe we have been challenged to accomplish in the name of Jesus, and I want you to think about the question, "What have been the results?" I can tell you, the result for each of us in this regard has been failure. Maybe not at the same rate or place or degree, but all of us ultimately experience failure, when accomplishing EVERYthing is the goal.

The bottom line is that we cannot accomplish EVERYthing, nor does God expect us to do so. If God realizes that we are never going to be enough, why does that discovery become so difficult for us to experience?

CHAPTER 1

We Will Never Be *Efficient* Enough

Proverbs 3:5-6

Early one morning, while sitting in the New Orleans International Airport, I made an amazing discovery: "The orange juice arrives in the middle of the night." You may not think this is as momentous a discovery as I did, but of course I was sitting in the airport in the middle of the night when I came to this important realization. (There was little else at the time to serve as entertainment!) As the squeak of the wheels of the orange-juice cart woke me from my sleep, part of me was just happy to see another living soul. I had come to the airport eight hours earlier to pick up my wife and daughters from a flight from Chicago. Because of bad weather, their flight from the Windy City continued to be delayed. Finally, they took off around 1:00 A.M. with a projected arrival time of 3:00 A.M.

Louis B. Armstrong Airport, the official name of the New Orleans International Airport, is a busy place for eighteen hours of the day, and it is considered to be one of the most-used airports in the country. For those other six hours late at night, however, things come to a screeching halt—with the exception of the orange-juice cart. Of course, I had never thought about it this way before—how each new day, travelers from around the world will descend upon the airport, some attending events in the city, some coming home, and others only passing through on their way to another destination. They will stop for breakfast, lunch, or dinner as they make deals by phone. They will grab snacks while they text-message and check their e-mails. They will prepare for the next "stage" of their life as they meet new people and say goodbye to old friends.

Apparently, they also will drink orange juice. It suddenly occurred to me on this occasion, that as the world goes by in its hustle and bustle, and while folks grab their orange juice on their way to the important events of life, someone is responsible, at 2:15 in the morning, for bringing the orange juice to the kiosk. It wasn't the pilot, the flight attendant, the janitor, the parking attendant, the gate rep, the TSA officer, or even the terminal manager. No, at 2:15 in the morning, a gentleman charged with pushing the orange-juice beverage cart to its appointed place, at the appointed hour, did his job.

No matter how important our job may be, none of us can make sure everything is done. We simply are not that efficient. Of course, most of the time, no one will ask who is getting the job done. No, most people the next day will take their orange juice and simply take for granted how it got there. But without that 2:15 A.M. delivery of not just orange juice, but of all the beverages, folks would simply be thirsty.

Efficiency is a simple concept. It is the ability to expend the minimal amount of time and energy to get the job done. But the unstated facts of this definition are important. To allow for the "minimal" use of time and energy points to the fact that there is a limited amount of both to be used in our world. Given the nature of our time and space, and with relativity still a theory, we can be in only one place at one time, and to accomplish everything remains a physical impossibility. No one can be that efficient.

God understood this about us, not only in terms of the physical world, but also in regard to the emotional and spiritual capacities of our lives. Proverbs 3:5-6 is a perfect explanation of how God views our world and the understanding of how we are best when we learn to get beyond our own finite gifts and abilities.

> Trust in the LORD with all your heart
> and lean not on your own understanding;
> in all your ways acknowledge him,
> and he will make your paths straight. (NIV)

If we take a closer look at that passage, we learn several lessons.

First, we are most inefficient in our understanding of "why" we can't accomplish everything. From the beginning, when Eve believed the Adversary, the question has been "wouldn't you like to be your own god?" The notion that we can accomplish every-thing has been a "heart" issue, because it has been the primal tension between wanting to be our own god and actually allowing God to be that part of our lives God was meant to be and for which we were created from the beginning. The writer of Proverbs says, "Trust in the LORD with all your heart"—not part of your heart, or just at certain times, but with "all your heart."

Second, this passage tells us, "Lean not on your own under-standing." Eve's propensity to believe the lie was to trust her own understanding first. She saw the truth, the answer to Satan's question, from her own limited point of view. God knows that we are most inefficient because we cannot know everything, and certainly we cannot understand the full scope of all the issues we encounter. Thus, God entreats us to "lean not on [our] own understanding."

Have you ever seen someone grow frustrated when he or she cannot get the answer to a question? I'm sure we all have been in that situation. The result often is that not only do we still not get the answer, but sometimes we also grow angry and make rash decisions that lead to other frustrations in our lives.

Instead, the writer of Proverbs says, "In all your ways acknowl-edge [God]." In other words, stop trying to be the final answer, and admit that you are unable to answer or know or understand every-thing. Look what happens next: When we do this, the writer says, then basically we are able to get out of our own way, and God is able to take the confusing, crooked paths of our lives and make them straight. I love this part, because it is such practical advice.

Think, for instance, of a man who is lost but won't stop and ask for directions. The result is one of two possibilities. Eventually, he will miraculously find the way or he will become so lost that there is no choice but to ask for help. What happens in the meantime? It is not pretty. There is a lot of anger and frustration that happens in working our way through a period of lostness. In these times, we are most aware of our inefficiency. Most important, we wander our way through life. If someone were to chart our path over the course of those experiences, the map might look like a bow tie, with many turns and twists. That is not God's intention for our life. God wants our paths to be straight.

CHAPTER 2

We Will Never Be *Versatile* Enough

1 Corinthians 15:58

Thank You's

Martin is shy and introverted. He is also incredibly kind. A nurse by trade, Martin works for a medical supply company and spends most of his time traveling from one clinic to another making sure doctors have the right equipment. He forces himself to be personable, though he would much rather be at home with a good book or spending time with his wife.

Martin's life has been filled with many obstacles, including family problems and broken relationships that for many years kept him far from church and from God. When Martin was in his late twenties, God sent a series of individuals into his life to help teach, heal, and guide him through the next paths and journeys. What Martin experienced was a much closer walk with God and, although such an introverted spirit, an incredible love for sharing his faith with others. Martin also became active in various mission projects and teams, including trips to Central America and ministries for the under-resourced in his local community.

I met Martin while serving part-time at a local church as the teaching pastor for the modern service. Immediately, I was drawn to his humble and gentle spirit. Several weeks after meeting Martin, he told me of a dream he had had a few days earlier that had made a profound impact on his spirit. (The dream was much like one the Apostle Peter had; see Acts 10:1–11:18.) However, unlike Peter's dream, Martin's dream was not about evangelism but about thankfulness. It started a chain of events in Martin's life that made me reconsider the way I say "thank you" to those I love.

In his dream, Martin was standing in an open field, looking up to heaven. Coming down from heaven a chain had been lowered. It was strong and shiny and well kept. The chain was both sturdy and beautiful—"not your run-of-the-mill chain," Martin kept saying. The chain was connected to Martin on one end and to heaven on the other. It was being used as a tether to keep Martin balanced and stable in the storms of life, and throughout the dream Martin saw one instance after another where the trouble and disappointments of life would blow through, but the chain would hold him steadily in place. Though the winds raged, Martin remained stable and in place.

Martin said that the chain was a source of great peace and encouragement, because it was a symbol for how he was connected to God and for how God would never let him go. Another interesting thing about the chain was that on each link was written the name of someone whom Martin had known in his life. On one link was the name of Martin's grandmother. On another, the name of his long-time Sunday school teacher. On another link was the name of the pastor who had baptized Martin, and on another, the name of Martin's wife. Martin informed me that my name was on a link, and I remember feeling very proud and honored.

The point was that the image of how Martin was connected to heaven, and to God, was a chain whose links represented the people who had loved, taught, and cared for him over the years. No matter how strong or good or knowledgeable Martin had been throughout his life, he had trusted and counted (even when he didn't realize it) upon the strength of those relationships with loved ones and friends to hold him steady.

This is a beautiful image of how we are intimately connected to each other and of how the value of those relationships, created in the image of God, is more apt than what we can know.

Of course, the opposite is too often true. We find ourselves trying to be everything to everyone, especially within these most sacred relationships. But no one, not even a dedicated, faithful soul like Martin, can hold tight through the storms alone. It takes a person willing to connect to others and to trust that he or she alone is not enough, but that together we are.

What usually happens, though, is that we spend time trying to be versatile enough. Versatile? A friend of mine says that we are most successful when we learn to be the most flexible in life—in essence, when we learn to be versatile and adaptive. One person alone cannot assimilate the full scope of all the issues and difficulties that life will throw our way. It takes other links in the chain to give us the flexibility of movement and the response to handle what life throws our way.

I love the chain image, because so many people throughout my ministry have tried to handle life on their own, to the point that they become so rigid, not necessarily by choice but because they can field only one issue, mistake, opportunity, or relationship at a time. Think of one person, alone, being like a metal rod. Sure, there may be some flexibility, but it will never compare with what is found in a "chain"—many people together—with many links. Also, anchor that metal rod to the ground in a time of storm, and it will hold only for as long as the strength of the rod in its current form and structure can stand. In essence, it will be only as strong as it is flexible. A chain, on the other hand—well, it can move and yet still be anchored, as long as the connections on either end are sure and true.

Strong and Steady

That is why I love what Paul says in 1 Corinthians 15:58 as he finishes his comments to the church at Corinth:

> So, my dear brothers and sisters, be strong and steady, always enthusiastic about the Lord's work, for you know that nothing you do for the Lord is ever useless. (NLT)

The church to whom Paul is speaking has been through a great deal, much of it at its own hands. The result is a fractured church that has lost its way in many regards. Of course, Paul has scolded and rebuked the church members for many of their practices that have led them away from the basics of the faith. In these final words, though, Paul offers them words of hope and encouragement.

Basically, Paul says, "You can't do it alone. . . . You are not enough." He says, "Together, as brothers and sisters in Christ, you can be all you need. You will be strong enough and steady enough, and it will affect even your joy and relationships. But," and this was the most important part, "remember that what you do for God is useful. Useful enough and important enough not to take it for granted. Give it your attention, work together, enjoy the moment; but more than anything, don't miss the chance to be all that God needs for you to be."

Learning to work together brings three things that we cannot experience to the same degree alone. First, when we work together, we experience strength. I learned as a kid roaming the woods of South Mississippi that one stick, which most anyone could find lying in the woods, could be broken with enough sawing, pulling, beating, or ingenuity. But tie six, seven, or eight sticks together into a bundle, and you change the dynamic dramatically.

Second, when we work together, we experience a steady spirit. A mountain-climbing friend of mine once explained the unique silence of the mountain at night. He said it was one of the most beautiful sounds you would ever want to experience . . . for a short time. To have that be your only existence, however, would be another story. Our spirits are wired to need other people. We are meant to bend and go with the flow, but ultimately our DNA is meant to respond to interactions with others. The Greeks called it *perichoresis*, the need for humanity to be engaged. When talking about the Trinity, the early Christian theologians borrowed the term to describe how the Father, Son, and Holy Spirit need one another. We understand this form of life, this intrinsic need for others, because deep down, it is how God has formed us. Without it, we are unsteady, out of balance, off our game.

Third and finally, when we work together, we find joy. We are meant to have joy. Jesus prayed for it. So did Paul. So did Peter when he talked about the early church. I believe that most churches in the United States today do not have enough joy.

Several years ago, there was a church that was about to split over whether the sanctuary walls should be painted. Yes, you heard me right. They were going to shut the doors of the church because they could not agree as to whether to *paint the walls*.

A friend of mine who is a church superintendent called me and asked if I would serve as the mediator in the conversation to resolve the problem. When I arrived, I found a long table with one group, the "pro-painters," as I called them, on one side, and the "anti-painters" on the other. They were sitting there, as I was a few minutes late, just staring at each other. I noticed two people at the end of the table carrying on casual conversation across the magic dividing line, but I later learned that they were the secretary and pastor of the church.

I sat listening for nearly forty-five minutes as the pro-paint group discussed the obvious need to paint the sanctuary. It had been nearly thirty years since the sanctuary had been painted. I had looked at the sanctuary, and, yes, it was in need of some improvements. Of course, so was the entire church facility, which had seen its better days. I believe the pro-paint group missed the mark in thinking that painting the walls would make a difference in whether people attended church or not. But that was a different argument.

The anti-paint group was basically from one family. Seven of them were sitting there. Two were brother and sister, while the rest were cousins or in-laws. "Our father painted that sanctuary by himself thirty years ago when no one else would step up and do it," the daughter said. "To paint over it would be a slap in his face." She was impassioned and real about her emotions, and it hit me that this was one of the last things that connected her to her father.

What really needed to happen was to get the walls painted as cheaply as possible, using volunteer labor, and then move on to a more significant project, such as feeding the hungry or taking care of the poor. Instead, here we were, debating whether to paint the sanctuary while in the meantime, as studies tell us, 14,000 children around the world were dying from not having enough food and water.

I squelched my indignation and heard the cases presented on both sides. Finally, I asked what seemed like a simple question, but one that from the moment it was asked I could tell had not been addressed before.

"Why did your father paint the sanctuary thirty years ago?" I asked.

The children looked at each other. They had not really thought about that question or the reason.

"Did he ever say why he felt the need to paint the sanctuary, especially by himself?" I asked again.

Finally, the brother, who had been silent throughout most of the debate, said, "He told me once that . . ." his voice trailed off. I could tell that he had heard the answer to his own realization of what I was asking, and why. He continued, "He told me once that it needed it. The trustees were fighting over whom they would get to paint it. While they fussed, my father bought the paint, set up the scaffolding, and did the work."

The rest of the group sat silent for a moment. No one, absolutely no one, had asked the next obvious question. Finally, I did: "What would your father say about this conversation today?" The sister eventually spoke up and said, "He would probably be in there painting the sanctuary."

Yes, he would.

The complexities of our world arise when, through action or deed, we prevent the body of Christ from working together. Through our petty actions or words or thoughts, we decide that we can do it, or at least control it, on our own. Neither is true. The real case is that we are in need of the fellowship that comes from working together to check and balance our perceptions of why and how something must be done, as much as we are in need of it in actually making things happen.

Not only do we not have the physical capacity, but also neither do we have the emotional or spiritual capacity to facilitate alone the full measure of what God wants us to do. God's work is useful because God makes it so and because, in us, we have the privilege to experience the very best of our gifts being used in tandem with others'. Only together are we versatile enough for any issue we might face.

CHAPTER 3

We Will Never Possess Enough *Expertise*

1 Peter 4:10

Dark, Stormy Nights

Several years ago, my wife and I had finished a presentation at a small, rural church in southwest Mississippi. The pastor was a friend of ours and had asked for us to speak to his congregation about our story. Of course we agreed, and we had a wonderful time. However, the trip required nearly two hours of travel on dark, two-lane roads through very small communities that rolled up the streets just after sundown. So as we made our way back home, we knew that the journey would be lonely and dark.

About thirty minutes into the return trip, a deer darted in front of our car, causing me to run off the right side of the road in order to miss hitting the animal. We missed the deer but caught the edge of two metal engine parts left on the side of the road from a previously broken-down car. The pieces were small in size but were jagged and strong enough to rip holes in both tires on the right side of our car, as well as send themselves rising up through our car's engine, nicking several hoses and belts. Within a matter of minutes, we were stranded on the side of the road with two flat tires and a damaged engine. We were also in the middle of nowhere with no cell phone coverage in the dark of night. On top of that, it was raining. No, it was not a good moment.

As I walked around the car, I realized that there was little I could do to help my situation. I knew how to change a tire, but I didn't know what to do with two flat tires. Although I had learned the parts of a car engine in my one year of industrial arts in high school, I couldn't make sense of the various fluid, steam, and smoke now spewing from my engine. And no matter how well known I had become in the course of my television ministry, it really didn't matter, stranded in the dark of night in a rainstorm in an area of the state whose people probably could care little about me being on television.

I told my wife later, I had never felt so useless in my life. Trying to flag down a passing car seemed like one of our few options, along with maybe finding someone who lived nearby who could help us. We took our "road safety kit" out of the trunk, set up our caution markers, and then started walking down the road to find some help. Eventually we came upon a house set back some distance in the woods. There was a single porch light on, and it seemed as though the residents were neither prepared for nor happy about visitors. We walked up to the house anyway.

After knocking on the door, I stepped back, remembering the countless movies I had seen where people "fired first and asked questions later." To my relief, the door opened (halfway, with the chain on the side) as an older gentleman, his wife standing behind him, answered the door and gruffly asked, "What do you want?" I explained about the car, the tires, and the engine, and about the church where I had just spoken (I thought the "preacher angle" might help). It wasn't until my wife, Pokey, stepped out from behind me, however, her hair and clothes soaked, that the older couple let down their guard a bit. Even looking like a drowned rat, Pokey is precious and beautiful, and the couple took an immediate liking to her.

They invited us in and allowed us to make phone calls for a wrecker that would take our broken-down vehicle and us back to our hometown. Of course, the trip cost me a fortune, but I didn't care. I just wanted "out of the woods" and back to the safety of our house.

I realized through that episode that as much as I knew and as much as I felt competent, even highly proficient, in so many areas of life—theology, writing, and organizational leadership—little of that helped me when the metal started flying through my tires and my engine. No matter what I knew, I wasn't expert enough for this situation.

A friend of mine who worked for a member of the U.S. House of Representatives recalls a trip he took to observe election results in a volatile-but-recovering African nation. The trip went well, he said, until rebels from the high country broke through the defenses along the city perimeters and began to attack forward into the safer districts of the area, including where the U.S. consulate was established.

Now, my friend is a genius. No kidding. He has multiple degrees from an Ivy League school. He is also quite a physical specimen: he looks like a professional athlete. As he said, though, when the mortar shells began to land around the courtyard of the consulate, there was little of his Ivy League training that could help him. He and his staff found themselves trapped in an office on the third floor of the consulate, with rebels gaining ground, even breaking through the north gate of the compound. The gunfire drew closer, and he actually feared that he and the other members of his group were about to be killed or taken hostage.

All of a sudden, four Marines crashed through the windows and secured the open doorway. One of them handed my friend a firearm (as if he knew what to do with it) and then began to escort the group to the window, where they were hoisted to the roof for a waiting helicopter. Eventually the entire group was flown from the roof to a nearby secure airport, where they then were flown to South Africa for safety.

My friend is one of the most capable people I have ever known. He is smart, good-looking, and talented, and he can write a mean speech or whip your tail in a game of one-on-one basketball. But even with all that he could do, there is a limit to his expertise. He needed those Marines to crash through the windows and rescue him.

Sometimes the reason we must learn to work together is because we are simply not expert enough to make the call or navigate the turn in some situations in which we find ourselves. And, yes, sometimes, all of us need someone to rescue us.

Nine Intelligences

I love the work of Howard Gardner. Howard Gardner is a Harvard professor who spent his life looking at how people were intelligent. Gardner realized that the question is not "How smart are you?" but "How are you smart?" His groundbreaking work revealed that everyone, including even some of our most challenged folks in society, has an "exceptionalized intelligence" that can be used in "the whole," if the whole will use it and value it.

Gardner narrows his list to nine different intelligences people can have. Some of them are in line with the more known, accepted forms of intelligences, such as language and mathematics. But others are intelligences related to interpersonal or intrapersonal abilities, whereby a person's primary gift may be in dealing with others or understanding themselves enough to make a real contribution to society.

This brings to mind for me words of the Apostle Peter, as he spoke to the members of the early Christian church:

> God has given gifts to each of you from his great variety of spiritual gifts. Manage them well so that God's generosity can flow through you.
>
> Are you called to be a speaker? Then speak as though God himself were speaking through you. Are you called to help others? Do it with all the strength and energy that God supplies. Then God will be given glory in everything through Jesus Christ. (1 Peter 4:10-11 NLT)

Howard Gardner's theory is reassuring because it reminds us that, as Peter said, every one of us has been gifted with something we do well, crafted for us from God's "great variety of spiritual gifts" for his children. It is a perfect system, if you think about it long enough. God has provided for the full scope of what the world might need to receive God's grace and plan for our lives. At the same time, God made the system itself the means by which the body of Christ, the fellowship of believers, rejuvenates itself, learns to love one another, values one another's abilities, celebrates our victories, and addresses our challenges together. One part of the system is practical and is used to accomplish God's plan. The other part is relational and is used to accomplish the purpose for God's children.

Both Gardner's theory and Peter's thoughts in his letter to the early Christians show us that none of us will have the needed expertise to accomplish everything. I might be a decent pastor and theologian, but that does not mean I can rebuild a car engine or patch a tire. Nor does it mean that a person who can understand the intricacies of public policy in third-world countries can, on the ground, rescue five people from attacking rebels. No, we are all in it together, and everyone is needed.

→ The idea that we can develop the expertise to accomplish everything is dangerous, delusional, and deceptive. The Adversary wants nothing more than to convince us that we are sufficient enough or, even worse, that we are deserving enough. How dangerous is that? Are you familiar with the biblical stories of Saul, David, Absalom, Solomon, Herod, or Judas? When we buy into that lie, something breaks at the most basic level of us and we become our own worst enemy.

Manage Them Well

At the close of Peter's letter to the early church, he reminds the followers that God had given each of them a gift, to be used according to God's purpose within the scope of what God had called them to do within that purpose. That all sounds a bit complicated, but here is the simple gist: God has given us a gift that fits within a greater plan for the whole of the body of Christ. We are to use it faithfully, for it is perfected when we use our gift for God's plan. But we are only one part of the plan. Everyone else's gifts matter too. Trying to be too much and do too much does several things. First, it devalues what God has given to us as our primary gift. Second, it disrupts the natural process of how God is working through us within the whole of the Body. Third, it decreases the effectiveness of God's plan because the focus remains on the "gift user" instead of the gift or the One who has given it.

It's true that some people are very gifted, multiply gifted, to great effect. But there is always a limit, and that limit can have great impact on the effectiveness of the Body, not just in getting the task accomplished, but also in experiencing the joy of getting the job done together.

So Peter's words of wisdom to us are to manage our gifts well. In other words, he is saying, "Don't overreach; don't try to be more than you should; don't try to be all things to all people. Simply do what you have been given to do to the best of your ability." Yes, in

some things, maybe even several, you will be an expert, an afi-
cionado. Don't forget, though, the strength of any chain is measured by the weakest of its links. How about your life? Knowing
your weak spots is part of your strength, part of knowing the full
scope of your potential. But, so many of us refuse to admit our
weak places or watch the chinks in the armor because of pride or
arrogance. Remember, though, what goes before the fall? It is not
knowledge, self-awareness, or honesty. It is pride.

Here is the dark side of this issue: when we work and work, putting ourselves out there for little in return, then our spiritual stam-
ina takes a hit. Just as with our bodies, our spiritual lives need the
refreshment of success and life and seeing what God is accomplishing in order to be rejuvenated and restored. When this doesn't
happen, we experience a serious case of spiritual burnout or even
physical and relational burnout. There is nothing more dangerous
to what God is doing in the world than for those who have
invested their lives heavily into God's plan to one day give up
because they believe they are out of steam or desire. We make ourselves the experts although we clearly have no business feeling this
way or doing these things. Ultimately, it will catch up with us.

CHAPTER 4

We Will Never Have Enough *Resources*

2 Corinthians 8:10-15

"What Can 50 Billion Dollars Buy?"

Someone asked this question of Bill Gates while he was attending a random Q&A session at a college campus. The person asking the question obviously was referring to the net worth of the world's richest man. It was a funny moment, because ultimately we learned that although Mr. Gates had $50 billion (yes, billion, with a "b") in the bank, he had no money in his wallet. In fact, he had so very little that, had he been dropped in somewhere by plane and forced to work his way home based on the cash on his person, he would have had to borrow money.

I don't remember how Mr. Gates actually answered the question. Some people in the audience had done the math and shared that, with his fortune, Bill Gates could buy untold numbers of houses, hundreds of thousands of prime real estate properties and acreage, and that he could spend so much (somewhere in the millions of dollars) every hour and never run out of money based on the interest earned on a simple certificate of deposit. It was staggering to see how much money Mr. Gates had and how much buying power one person exercised.

The next day, I saw a news report from Zimbabwe. The people of Zimbabwe have been in the midst of the worst economic crisis, possibly in the history of the world. Their inflation rate is in the tens of thousands of percent. Currently, the second-worst inflation rate is around 70 percent, and that is in post-war Iraq.

The news report pointed out that to buy two loaves of bread in Zimbabwe would cost—wait for it—50 billion Zimbabwe dollars. My eyes did a double take, and so did my brain. How in the world could one man use 50 billion American dollars to buy so much, compared to an entire nation being able to afford only two loaves of bread for 50 billion Zimbabwe dollars? The answer is a complex formula of economics that places value in many forms and figures, but in the end, whether you are Bill Gates or an entire nation, there is a limit to what your $50 billion will buy. Enter Warren Buffet. Mr. Buffet is also a billionaire whose fortune hovers around the $50 billion mark. Recently Mr. Buffet announced that he would give his estate to the Gates Foundation, to fight poverty. When asked why he would give away the bulk of his estate to a foundation and not to his children, he talked about how wealth and resources have a paralyzing effect on people, and he said that the best way for us to value the resources we have been given is to make them work for us for the good of the world.

Over the years, Mr. Buffet said, the plan is that his resources will be pooled with those of Mr. Gates to provide better school class-rooms, drinking wells, vaccines, new hospitals and clinics, and a host of other humanitarian endeavors. No list of houses or acreage needed; $50 billion will buy some peace of mind and improvement of living for millions of people in our world.

When Mr. Buffet and Mr. Gates formally announced their plans, the media had a field day. They talked about grand plans for how these gifts will make a huge difference in the world. Mr. Buffet credited Bill and Melinda Gates with inspiring his thinking for how to share his wealth to make a difference in the world. These plans, as mentioned above, are grand, and the scope is powerful.

At the end of the press conference, Mr. Gates and Mr. Buffet were asked one last question that received little coverage by the news media. It went something like this: how far does this gift go toward eradicating poverty and those conditions that so plague our humanity? Mr. Gates and Mr. Buffet looked at each other, and Mr. Gates answered, "Our gifts do only a small part in what is a massive need for resources and assistance." With that, the two men left the podium, and the conversation was over.

One man was worth $50 billion. The other was worth nearly $50 billion. But under different circumstances, between them, they could buy four loaves of bread in Zimbabwe.

There is a massive need for assistance in the world, and as much as these gifts mean in helping meet those needs, they represent only a small portion of the total amount of resources needed. Think about that. Ninety-four billion dollars represents only a small amount of what is needed. Certainly it is a significant start and a huge statement regarding what these two men are trying to accomplish. But as the situation in Zimbabwe and various other struggles and needs remind us, no one has enough resources to meet all of our world's needs. Mr. Gates can't do it. Neither can Mr. Buffet. Neither can Wal-Mart, General Electric, or Exxon-Mobil. Their contributions would be awesome starts. But they won't finish the job.

According to What One Has

The Apostle Paul says it best in his letter to the church at Corinth. Apparently the church had been arguing over the use of resources: those who had many resources were not sharing faithfully, and those who had few were being made to feel as though they did not matter. Paul settled both issues. He said that no matter how much a person has, a person can never have enough; no matter what a person does not have, that person will never have too little to participate and contribute in making a difference. The passage is clear. Paul says,

> Here is my advice about what is best for you in this matter: Last year you were the first not only to give but also to have the desire to do so. Now finish the work, so that your eager willingness to do it may be matched by your completion of it, according to your means. For if the willingness is there, the gift is acceptable according to what one has, not according to what he does not have.
>
> Our desire is not that others might be relieved while you are hard pressed, but that there might be equality. At the present time your plenty will supply what they need, so that in turn their plenty will supply what you need. Then there will be equality, as it is written: "He who gathered much did not have too much, and he who gathered little did not have too little." (2 Corinthians 8:10-15 NIV)

Paul's message here is not just about the use of resources, but about the nature of where resources fit within the overall scope of God's plan. Paul is clear that resources are tools for making the Kingdom come to fruition. He says that it takes everyone to make the process work the way God intends, not because of the amount, but because of how "working together" provides a new sentiment toward resources and community in general. For Paul, the real lesson here is about equality.

When those who have much share what they have and those who have less or little share what they have, Paul says that we are "supplying" one another's needs by working to share and build equality among ourselves. Further, he says that we are valued or measured not in amounts, but by our participation in the mission of the Kingdom.

This is not the first time Jesus or the apostles confronted this issue. Jesus talked about it in discussing the widow's mite and the young man who brought the fishes and the loaves.

The story of fulfilling our potential is not about wealth. So often we convince ourselves that we can navigate life based on what we have instead of relying on God's provisions. However, as we learn from Paul's message to the church at Corinth, and as we see in the examples of the widow who gave what little she had for the offering and the boy who shared his five loaves of bread and two fish to feed a crowd of thousands, it is understanding what we do not have that provides the potential for accomplishing great things. We are a people who work not from our abundance, but from our poverty. We are not enough. But God is.

Marie

Marie is one of my favorite people, whose joy for life is both infectious and beautiful to watch. She also teaches me about getting the most from every moment and about never taking anything for granted.

Marie had just gotten her first paycheck ever, and she was giddy with excitement. In fact, I had never seen her so happy. As she waved the paper in front of me, I could tell this was no ordinary day. She kept motioning to it, and eventually I saw the pay stub, with her name printed on the front. "Are you going to take me to dinner?" I asked. She smiled and nodded. I continued, "Well, you tell your mom to set a date, and we will celebrate." Marie walked toward her mother, and, having heard our conversation, her mother confirmed that we would set a dinner date to celebrate Marie's big day. Never mind that the check was for only $1.78. To Marie, it seemed like a million dollars.

I had met Marie seven years earlier when she and her family arrived at the local community center for one of the first worship services in our new congregation. Growing up Catholic, Marie and her family were members of a sister parish in the neighboring town, but they had been looking for a church closer to home. When friends told Marie's father about our new congregation, the family decided to visit. For all of us, it was "friendship at first sight." They joined our church within a matter of weeks.

For years now I have shared that story, and how Marie and her family profoundly affected my life. In spite of the many struggles I face, it wasn't until I met Marie that I became truly aware of God's unbelievable, yet abundant grace. Marie sees the world differently from most of us. She is not self-centered. She finds joy in simple things. She loves hearts, stuffed animals, and an afternoon swim. Marie accepts everyone, and even if you don't want or like it, she hugs you, forcing you to drop your protective cloak and bask in the precious vulnerability that is real life. Marie is a champion for authentic relationships, fragility, and expectation; and she never apologizes for being so.

To say that Marie makes an impression is an understatement. From the moment she enters a room, she receives attention because of her electric smile and engaging personality. But there are other noticeable traits about Marie, for she also has cerebral palsy, a condition said to be created in her case from a disrupted umbilical cord at birth. She communicates nonverbally, and although she can walk, she has pronounced mobility issues. For some people, Marie's presence is very difficult. A sense of awkwardness and silent pity fill many as they struggle to find the words to explain or excuse their discomfort.

However, people's reactions do not concern Marie. Although she is a young woman now, her demeanor and interaction remind you of a small child. She approaches others with a deep innocence, as though every person she meets is a unique gift from God. In spite of a person's awkwardness or difficulty in dealing with her condition, Marie shows none of that awkwardness in return. Actually, moments after meeting her, she can lead even the most caustic person to feel at ease, not only with her, but also, as many have told me later, with themselves as well.

Marie finds joy in simple things and, in the process, helps others experience their own value. This is why a simple paycheck instilled in her such a sense of excitement and pride. No matter the amount of the paycheck, it was hers, and that was enough.

Marie teaches lessons about self-perception that many find impossible to learn. She simply meets people where they are and finds the best in all situations. When Marie looks at her world, she does not see limitations or the usual inhibitions that keep us from one another or God, and she does not form defenses that keep her invulnerable to those around her. On the contrary, Marie uses each day as an opportunity for discovery, to find a new treasure along her path. She is content with what she has and is convinced that what she has is exactly what she needs. O, that we would be so blessed!

CHAPTER 5

We Will Never Possess Enough *Yearning*

Matthew 6:19-21

Veggies in a Pill

Growing up, I hated to eat my vegetables. In fact, most of my "green intake" consisted of apple-flavored Jolly Ranchers! I knew that vegetables were important to my diet, and as I grew older and became a father, I did better, usually choking down one vegetable or another, mostly with the help of a rich sauce that only negated the nutritional value of the vegetable itself. No matter how much someone told me the benefits of eating my vegetables, I struggled to find the value in them. Eventually I tolerated broccoli and sugar snap peas. But you could chase me around the house with carrots or regular green peas and still I wouldn't eat them. Vegetables just weren't my "cup of tea." I even tried a concoction that said you could get your vegetables by drinking certain herbal teas. The only problem is that the tea tasted like boiled-down vegetables!

I kept wondering, with all of the technology we have in this world, why couldn't someone invent a pill that would cover the nutrients and necessities for eating our vegetables? One day someone answered my question. My wife first brought "Veggies-in-a-pill" home after our second daughter was born. The pills were large and green and had an interesting odor about them that reminded you of—you named it—vegetables. There was also a "Fruits-in-a-pill" version that was a red caplet and, true to form, smelled like fruit. I found that if you took them together, the fruit smell overcame the veggie smell. The problem was, you had to take three pills three times per day for both the vegetables and the fruits. That's a lot of pill-taking.

One day, while complaining about the amount of pills we had to take, my wife quickly pointed out that it was either take the pills or eat the vegetables, to which I replied that was not really a choice, but rather the choice of one evil over another. I kept taking the pills.

We did this for about a year, until the next brand of "veggies-in-a-pill" arrived, this time looking like a Gummi bear and tasting like candy. Now, that's my idea of a vegetable—a candy Gummi bear that smells like fruit. I don't mind getting my daily intake of Brussels sprouts and carrots that way at all.

Yes, I know I sound like a picky eater, but I am not quite as bad as I am making myself out to be. My mother would certainly be disappointed by my poor characterization of vegetables, and I know my grandmother would lecture me on how vegetables from the ground were all they had to eat during the Great Depression. So, yes, I ate my vegetables; but given the choice, I would not have. Hey, I am just trying to be honest!

My take on vegetables reminds me that, although I like many different kinds of foods, I will never like all kinds of foods. I like most meats, including pork, chicken, duck, beef, venison—you name it. I'll even eat most casseroles (including the ones with vegetables). My dining habits do not prevent me from trying new things or even eating beyond my culture or comfort zone. Given my druthers, however, I would rather not eat a lot of veggies. It's nothing personal; they are just not part of my natural yearning for foods.

Life is like that, too. We are not born to like everything. We don't all like the same music. We don't like the same TV shows. We don't like the same movies or books. We don't like the same foods. Given those differences, it is not surprising that we don't all like the same tasks for doing good and the same projects for serving.

Each of us has been gifted to like certain things. We all yearn for something.

I call it "the keep-you-up-at-night syndrome." There are moments when God gets my attention so completely, so directly, that I know who is speaking and that I need to listen. These "moments with God" are about specifics, whereby I feel personally connected to what God is doing in the world. It might be a service project in my local community or a reach to orphans halfway around the world. Regardless, when God begins to tug at my heart, I know that I must answer.

One Woman's Love

Several years ago, I had the opportunity to meet a wonderful South African woman named Gutti; her birth name is very long and difficult to say properly, so she preferred this shorter, easier name. Gutti had been a nurse in one of the larger towns in South Africa and had, from an early age, had many advantages not afforded to other women in her village. This included her sisters who remained in the local village and who had saved their meager earnings to send their younger sister to the academy to be trained as a nurse. They had chosen Gutti to "make it." The sisters did not have much of a life themselves, but through their baby sister they could see someone in their family succeed.

Gutti left the village, received her training as a nurse, and proceeded to spend several years working in the hospitals of Johannesburg and other areas. One day she received a message from home that one of her sisters was dying. Gutti returned home just before her oldest sister died from complications due to AIDS. Her sister's husband had gone into the city, been involved with a prostitute, and not told his wife. His wife died of pneumonia a year after her husband succumbed to the effects of AIDS himself. They left behind four children.

Gutti decided to take the four children and raise them herself, especially when she realized that her other sisters were also infected with the AIDS virus, by the same means as her oldest sister. Their husbands too had had sex with infected partners and had not told their spouses. This is not uncommon in Gutti's village, but during her absence she had forgotten how badly women in general were treated in their society.

Over the next few years, all the rest of Gutti's sisters would die of the disease, leaving behind sixteen more children. Altogether, Gutti became the guardian to twenty nieces and nephews. At first Gutti wondered if she could take care of all the children. But as she would later share, God spoke to her in a dream and told her to "get up and care for these children."

Gutti not only moved back to the village to care for her nieces and nephews, she set up a clinic to take care of other HIV-positive patients and their families. Eventually Gutti's brood grew to more than forty children, as other orphans joined the ranks of her "family." As the news spread, though, that Gutti was taking care of orphans, strangers began to leave their children on her doorstep, and eventually she became overwhelmed with the sheer number of children she was caring for. Soon she had to put up a sign turning families away.

However, other families who lived near Gutti and who had watched her witness did not want the orphaned children to be abandoned; so they started taking in the children themselves. Where Gutti could not help any longer, the neighbors stepped in. Finally, the community created a neighborhood orphanage, and one family after another provided shelter and care for those in need.

Gutti's yearning to help was huge, unbelievably so. However, there was a limit to what she could do alone. When her yearning was connected to that of her neighbors, so many more were helped.

Our Treasures, Passions, and Yearnings

Jesus said, "Where your treasure is, there your heart will be also" (Matthew 6:21). Where our yearnings are, there too rests our greatest potential, because it is in these places that we can't sleep, that our struggles bear upon us until we decide to fix them, and where our passions rule the day until we decide to confront the broken edges and make them whole again.

This passage, Matthew 6:19–21, has been quoted for so many purposes, especially for talking about our money, that we have become desensitized to it. The purpose behind this message, though, is not about our money. It is about what drives how we place value on our things and our goals in life. Jesus is perfectly right: real value is found in where and what our hearts desire.

However, just as there is a limit to our resources, there is also a limit to the passions that drive how we spend our money, how we use our time, and how we use our gifts. We will never have a yearning or a passion for everything. Some things keep me up all night, whereas when it comes to other issues, I sleep like a baby!

Most people know that Babe Ruth was one of the greatest hitters in baseball history. For years he led the Major Leagues in home runs, hits, and slugging percentage. The numbers he put up are astounding, especially in an age when baseball was mostly about advancing one base at a time.

What some people don't know is that Babe was also an outstanding pitcher. In fact, many believe that he could have had just as wonderful a career had he remained a pitcher; and for a while in his career, he did both, pitching and hitting. Ultimately, he had to make a choice as to which one he would focus on—continue to pitch, or move into the outfield on defense and concentrate on hitting. The decision was made by Babe himself (with a little help from his coach). When he was asked which one he had more passion for, he responded, "I like to hit the ball a long way." Babe stayed with hitting, and the rest is history.

God has given us a yearning for something special in our lives. Some call it passion; others call it spiritual gifts. Some may even call it their burden. Regardless of the name, the Bible is clear that we are to take that area of our life and live it to the fullest, doing whatever is necessary to be the best and to share that gift with the world. But we don't have a passion for everything. Nor do we have the spiritual gifts to live out all of our passions and yearning; that is not how we are "wired up." Instead, God has a bigger plan.

The Bigger Plan

God's bigger plan is that everyone will do what he or she has been called and gifted to do—nothing more, nothing less. In living out those yearnings, those passions, we are able to confront the world's troubles.

I learned this from my friend Jack, who showed me a map of how his organization had targeted several areas in the countries where they were in ministry. In each country, he listed the government-run hospitals. They were sparse and covered only a small percentage of the area. Then he added in nonprofits, Red Cross stations, and so on. These were more substantial in number, but nowhere near what was needed. Then my friend added to the map all of the churches at work; they covered the entire area of each country.

The "bigger plan" is that God has gifted us to care and to be cared for within the framework of brothers and sisters, who all have their own passions, yearnings, and gifts for making a difference in the world. No one can be enough; but together, we will be more than sufficient.

Okay, so it is clear that "We can't do EVERYthing." That seems pretty self-explanatory now. I suspect you already knew it. (But thanks for humoring me along the way!)

Yet, we can do "SOMEthing" to change our world and to make a difference in the great gulf between our homes and the ends of the earth, much like the Great Commission says (Matthew 28:18-20). Life is more significant when people with different interests work together to share the load and to use their talents and gifts more effectively. There is no magic pill. Each person is driven by a non-negotiable area of passion taken from God's heart and planted in ours. The idea is simple, but it works; and it has worked for thousands of years.

In the chapters and pages that follow, you will see how you can help, how you can make a difference, change your life, change someone else's life, have an impact upon your community, and affect your world. More than anything, I believe you will see that God has already shown up, that God is already at work, and wants to take the best of what God has planted inside of you and make it work.

PART II

". . . So Do SOMEthing"

The Lighthouse

In late 2004, the church I founded and where I served as senior pastor for nearly a decade dedicated a family missions center called The Lighthouse. The name was chosen from a congregational survey and vote. I'll admit the name was not my favorite, but the congregation loved it.

The name was meant to convey the purpose of the facility, which was built by the congregation to minister to the under-resourced persons of the community through a food pantry, a clothes closet, life skills programs, and various other ministries designed to help give people dignity, hope, healing, and a new direction as they navigate the jagged rocks of life.

Today, The Lighthouse provides food and services to literally hundreds of families per week and has become a powerful standard for hope in the small community I served. With all we accomplished over that decade together, I am most proud of how the people loved each other and, especially, how they loved "the least of these," as Jesus said (Matthew 25:40), their neighbors, brothers, and sisters in greatest need.

However, as with so many things, with The Lighthouse there was a story behind the story. The land where The Lighthouse sits was donated by a family whose members were new to the congregation. When we made the announcement that we were looking for a site to host our new family missions center, this particular family approached me and offered to donate a piece of land, slightly more than an acre, in one of the most under-resourced areas of the community. It was a perfect location for our mission.

The lot was not much to look at. Trees and brush had overgrown the front of the property, and at the back sat a concrete slab, long ago the foundation of the family's old home place.

It was also the site of a tragedy. The eldest daughter of the family, who was in charge of making arrangements for transferring the property to the church, told me the story of how their father, an abrupt, abusive man, had repeatedly beaten and tortured their mother, until their mother had found the strength to leave, taking the children with her.

The father continued to live in the house. Over the years, he would slip back and forth between drunken rages and short periods of lucid sobriety. The children did their best to care for him, but ultimately he would hurt them and would, with words and actions, do everything in his power to push them away. Then, days later, in the familiar pattern, he would beg them back into his life.

This pattern continued until the children were in college, where they found their own lives apart from their father's desperate, broken cycles. The eldest daughter remembered receiving a call one morning from her father, asking her to come by after she got out of class. At first she protested, but after much pleading from her father, eventually she promised to be at the house around noon.

Little did she know that her father was asking her to come home for more than a visit and to witness an unspeakable horror. When she arrived, her father, standing in the doorway of the house, had soaked himself as well as the porch and the rest of the home in gasoline. When the daughter began walking from her car to the porch, she watched her father light a match and set himself on fire. The house exploded into flames, and in an instant, her father and the house were gone. Only days later, the remnants of the house were demolished.

For nearly two and a half decades, the family completely left the property alone, as it became covered in the debris of foliage, legend, and bad memories. They refused to do anything with it, never agreeing whether to sell it or rebuild it. The property simply sat there for nearly twenty-five years as a symbol of horror, pain, suffering, and hopelessness.

Thus, it was all the more remarkable that the family, hearing our need for a site for our new missions center, would discuss among themselves and agree that God was moving them to give the property to the church. As the eldest daughter signed over the deed to the church, she said, "We agree that the devil has had this property long enough. It is now time for God to do something beautiful with it."

Later that afternoon, several of us from the missions center team gathered with the family and took a picture of the newly mowed property. We held our shovels to break ground on a place that would ignite a new kind of fire, one born from the heart and grace of God.

That evening after the festivities, the mother of the family came by my house with a gift. It was a large square box that I could tell had been stored away for many years. She left it at the door with a note taped to the side. The note read: "In this box is the only thing we were able to save from the rubble of the house after the fire. I have had it in my attic all of these years, waiting to see what God would do next. We have prayed that God would transform our pain into something that could be helpful for those who have been battered and beaten by life. I hope you enjoy it."

I took the box, placed it on the dining room table, and opened it. What I pulled out was a worn-but-beautiful oil painting, still in a gold-leaf frame but with black soot marks along the edges. As I turned the painting around to look at the front, the image literally caused me to lose my breath. It was a picture of a lighthouse.

There are no coincidences in God's plan.

There is a plan, whether we want to admit it or not. God is at work to redeem the world and to put back together a broken relationship between God and God's people. Of course, that brokenness has poured over into the relationships among God's people as well. That is evident in an extreme way in how a father and husband could stand in a doorway and kill himself as his daughter walks up the driveway. God is working to redeem even those unreasonable, unexplainable situations.

Over the years of shame and grief associated with their father's act, the children who owned the property where The Lighthouse was established first ignored the area like it was condemned or laced with nuclear waste. Then they searched for something, anything that might just rid them of the memories. They had long given up on the idea of the pain going away or the situation being redeemed for some greater meaning. When the idea arose of donating the land for use to the most under-resourced of our community, however, the Holy Spirit gave the family a word that transformed their grief into possibility. Certainly their gift of the land was not enough by itself; the center still had to be built, funds had to be raised to operate the center, and many other such considerations. But their gift was *something*, and that something was a place and a story that would never be forgotten.

> Follow the way of love and eagerly desire spiritual gifts, especially the gift of prophecy. For anyone who speaks in a tongue does not speak to men but to God. Indeed, no one understands him; he utters mysteries with his spirit. But everyone who prophesies speaks to men for their strengthening, encouragement and comfort. (1 Corinthians 14:1-3 NIV)

In 1 Corinthians 14, the Apostle Paul provides instruction for the early Christian believers to be focused in the gifts that the Lord has given them in order to build up the body of believers. Paul is also clear that not every gift is for every situation and that we have been gifted to serve faithfully no matter what the situation or how we may grow to feel about it. This is not easy. But Paul understands, maybe better than any of us, that serving and using our gifts requires real faithfulness, focus, and a certain fortitude in order for our gifts to be used appropriately and consistently and to make a difference in our world. Just as we must realize that we are incapable of accomplishing *everything* the world might need from us, we must be just as diligent in using the gifts that we know God expects us to use.

The following chapters discuss how we make use of the SOMEthing that God has gifted each of us with and how that gift can change our communities and our world. There is no miracle answer for how God uses our gifts. It requires hard work and faithfulness, as well as the work and community of others who are doing the same with their gifts. But that is the very nature of the body of Christ working together. When that SOMEthing in each of us is developed faithfully, implemented appropriately, and held to account by others whom we trust and with whom we make the journey, the potential is limitless.

I would be remiss not to mention that the opposite is also true. The level by which we miss the mark and underachieve our potential is directly responsible for how our gifts are implemented and how that effectiveness is experienced and felt.

My friends who gave the property to be used for The Lighthouse center did not see that act necessarily as a watershed spiritual moment. They simply wanted to do SOMEthing with the gift they had in order to resolve the shame and guilt of the past years associated with their father's suicide, to allow Christ to restore their situation, and to give hope to the family's future. Most of our gifts are not so dramatic as this family's donation, but they can be equally powerful because God needs only one willing soul to recalibrate the potential of any situation.

CHAPTER 6

We Must *Sacrifice*

Romans 12:1-3

Ms. Hattie

Ms. Hattie worked as a housecleaner, seamstress, and laundry maid her entire life. She worked hard and long hours. Her employers lived in another part of town. Ms. Hattie arrived to work early, accommodating the wealthy members of her community. When she returned home, she took care of her own family—six of them, three boys and three girls. Ms. Hattie's husband had died while their youngest child was still a baby. There was no rest for Ms. Hattie; there was no other choice.

According to the world's standards, Ms. Hattie never had much. However, she always had a smile, and a belief that with just enough hard work and sacrifice, anything was possible. Although Ms. Hattie had little to offer in terms of material things, she taught her children rich lessons about God, family, and working hard. Through her family, Ms. Hattie created a wealth beyond any the world could measure or define.

Her first child was accepted to a small liberal arts college in South Carolina. Her second child earned a scholarship to Vanderbilt University. Her third child, the oldest son, made the Ivy League and went off to Brown University. Her fourth and fifth children, twins, attended a large university in the northern part of their state. Her sixth child? Well, he went to Harvard.

How does a seamstress send six kids to college? Through a life surrendered in sacrifice toward higher goals than the comforts this world affords. Such is the doorway to significance.

Ms. Hattie said that she learned sacrifice from her maternal grandmother, who was also a seamstress and the first generation of her family living out of slavery. Ms. Hattie's grandmother used hard work as an opportunity to give her family dignity and to provide the needed resources to "inch herself" ever closer to more and more opportunity. It may not have seemed like much at the time, and it certainly did not happen quickly; but over time, Ms. Hattie's grandmother taught her valuable lessons about the giving of yourself for a purpose much greater than your own interests. Ms. Hattie passed those lessons down to her children.

Ms. Hattie loves to tell the story of two of her cousins who wanted to get rich quick. One got into "moonshine," and the other got involved in various forms of gambling. Both of them ended up without families who loved them and without any real success except the occasional "hit." The "hits" were few and far between, and both of her cousins died lonely and broke.

Ms. Hattie was a different story. Not only did she raise a family whose witness outshone that of most others around them, but her children understood the value of life and how to manage the "things" they accumulated. They viewed the world through their mother's eyes, no matter what academic degrees they received or how much money they made. Thus, they invested in the virtue of sacrifice too, and they passed it to their children.

As Ms. Hattie's health began to fail, several of her children invited her to come live with them. Being a homebody, however, she chose to remain in the little community where she was born and had lived her whole life. Her children tried to get her to leave and join them, but she would always say, "I was born here, and I will die here."

Ms. Hattie died at the age of ninety-two. She still worked part-time as a seamstress, and she still was very active in her church. She also attended a local card game until just weeks prior to her death, and she continued to save her money and encourage others. When Ms. Hattie died, the local banker contacted her children and asked them to gather at the bank to discuss her will. "Will? *What* will?" people asked. No one was aware of any formal will. But Ms. Hattie was prepared.

Her will stated that 10 percent of her estate should go to her church. Now, Ms. Hattie had been in a running feud with the ladies and friends of her church for several decades, but it was all talk; in reality, they loved one another very much.

She gave another 10 percent of her estate to various community ministries, including her former high school, whose administrators used the gift Ms. Hattie left them to start a new library fund.

Finally, she left the other 80 percent of her estate to a local shelter ministry. Her children did not receive any funds, and, per-haps not surprising, none of them protested. They had been told early on what their mother was planning to do, and she had reminded them that her gift to them over the years was love and an opportunity.

The remarkable part of the entire process was that the estate was valued at nearly $400,000. No one knew that Ms. Hattie had saved that much money—well, no one but her banker and her pastor. They both watched Ms. Hattie live a life of frugality so that one day others might benefit. When her television broke, she saved for more than a year to pay for repairs to fix it. When she needed new shoes, she wore the old ones until, literally, the soles fell off. When she needed a dress for some event, instead of buying a new one, she would wear the same hand-mended dress she had worn for years.

Ms. Hattie gave her life as a holy and living sacrifice, and she wanted her resources to count for something more than the next purchase or for the next "want." One of her attorneys remarked after her death, "Ms. Hattie could have lived a completely different life than she had known, but instead, she chose to live her life in her manner. The result was a very wealthy life, not measured by money but by the kind of wealth the world cannot take away." How true that is.

Ms. Hattie's example for all of us is that her SOMEthing began with sacrifice wrapped in a life that held others to account; but more than anyone, she held herself to account for how she valued her world, how she used her resources, and how she treated others.

The Romans 12 Bombshell

> Therefore, I urge you, brothers, in view of God's mercy, to offer your bodies as living sacrifices, holy and pleasing to God—this is your spiritual act of worship. Do not conform any longer to the pattern of this world, but be transformed by the renewing of your mind. Then you will be able to test and approve what God's will is—his good, pleasing and perfect will.
>
> For by the grace given me I say to every one of you: Do not think of yourself more highly than you ought, but rather think of yourself with sober judgment, in accordance with the measure of faith God has given you. (Romans 12:1-3 NIV)

When I was a little boy and my mother was trying to make a significant point, she would lay out her evidence for how or why I should act in a certain situation. It was usually a well-crafted argument followed by the consequences if I chose to comply or not. Her transition in the conversation to this part of the discussion always began with the word *therefore*. As soon as I heard that word, I knew we were getting close to the real purpose of the conversation. She would begin, "Therefore, you need to . . ." and usually we were well on our way to whatever task or conversation we needed to undertake.

This is what the Apostle Paul does in Romans 12 to set up the transition in the discussion from following the rules of the Christian faith to actually living the faith in our actions, relationships, and duties. What a transition it is! Paul says that we transform our lives by becoming holy and "living sacrifices." Now, this may not seem all that enticing an invitation to us today, because our understanding of the word *sacrifice* conjures up a variety of images—altars in darkened temples, pagan witch doctors standing over maidens before they are thrown into a volcano, or even poor defenseless animals given over to religious officials in order to assuage some angry god. No, the idea of *sacrifice* typically is not a modern-day motivator.

Paul's understanding of sacrifice is different, even within the context of his own time. To Paul, sacrifice was a gift given back to God without any strings attached. The sacrifice was whole: it didn't come in pieces or parts, but included the complete nature of the One who was giving it. In other words, you didn't hold back the good parts or the secret parts or the parts about which you weren't certain. No, *you gave all of the gift.* It was complete.

For Paul to say that we should present ourselves as "holy and living sacrifices" to God says much about how Paul sees our lives being used in service to Christ. The old manner of sacrifice was a process that had to be repeated often and was never sufficient for the long haul. Through Christ, though, Paul sees the potential of what God has done in us, and he knows that it is sufficient because it is our SOMEthing, planted deep within our spiritual DNA and validated by Christ's love for us. Heavy stuff? Yes! But *important* stuff nonetheless, because it takes us beyond our own selfish desires, and it defines our efforts and frames our lives within the will of God. This is "God's plan for us"—God's abiding gift—as long as we will accept it and move forward to live it. To Paul, this happens in several steps.

First, we *present* ourselves to God. This is something that we do because we love God and, more important, because we believe God loves us. We do it selflessly and without condition. It is our first choice among many, and it shows God where our hearts are. I have often told friends of mine who work for the church that our competition today is not the church of the other denomination down the street, but everything else a person can choose to do besides being in relationship with God. Our competition is all the other ways people can choose to spend their time and share their resources. Paul sees this as a wonderful way to make a statement for God at the beginning—to say, beyond any other words or actions, "I want to be with you."

Second, we present ourselves as *holy* and *living*. *Holy* is an interesting term, because it can mean so many things. For Paul, *holy* meant proximity, nearness, not only to present us to God but also to draw close to God and to all that God stands for in our lives. We want not only to be close to God in terms of distance, but also in terms of how our lives mirror what is important in the world. God not only wants us to walk *with* God, but to walk *like* God. If you want to do something significant for God, then learn God's ways, spend time in God's teachings, model your life after the life of Jesus Christ. In other words, *walk* and *talk* like him. These are the ways people see God in and through us and the means by which they know who God can be in their own lives.

This brings us to the word *living*. Most sacrifices in Paul's day were dead at the time they were given. They were remnants of what life used to be, whether it was the animal that lay on the altar or the discussions that took place among the priests as they executed one more ritual for a God they had long since forgotten how to describe and love. *Living* is a powerful word here, not because Paul is saying that you get to be "alive" while doing this, but because your presence and your holiness and your purpose *for* doing it are *alive* too. This is not a static gift or presentation, but the ongoing process of *relationship* that transforms the words on the page into real life. It also helps people caught up in ritual, whether it's the ritual of religion or the ritual of an everyday, meaningless life, to find some purpose again. For Paul, to present yourself as *living* was not just to present yourself as "undead" (which calls to mind mummies and vampires!); instead, it was to present yourself as *active, working, changing, transforming, transcending,* and *overcoming*. There is energy in this kind of life; and coupled with holiness, it is more complete, more whole, than anything the world can define.

When we present ourselves as *holy* and *living*, as Paul encourages, what are the results? Three things happen to us when we do this.

First, we please God. We say to God that our relationship with, through, and in God is the most important thing in our lives.

Second, we transform our patterns by renewing our minds and changing our habits. We no longer live the way the world lives because we see that there is a difference, and we no longer want to be shaped by something that does not draw us closer to God.

Third and finally, we recognize God's will in our lives and how God is working in us. It is like opening a door to a new destination, and although we may not be able to see the end clearly, we understand and trust the guide along the way.

Friends, this is a bombshell set against the world's plan and the way the world so often has seen itself—in contrast to how even religious people often have gone about their lives. There are no rules or rituals here, it is about *relationship* and about believing in something bigger than yourself that gets you up each day and drives you to make a difference.

Of course, this idea did not originate with Paul. He had heard all of this before in the teaching of the other apostles, who themselves had heard it before from Jesus and, most importantly, had seen it modeled in Jesus' example and life. Jesus was talking about sacrifice when he said, "For those who want to save their life will lose it, and those who lose their life for my sake will find it" (Matthew 16:25), and when he said, "The last will be first, and the first will be last" (Matthew 20:16). Sacrifice was and remains at the heart of the good news because it was and remains at the heart of Jesus.

Another Ms Hattie? Me? Really?

"I can't live like Ms. Hattie!" "I can't give away everything!" I have heard these sorts of comments my entire ministry. For many people, their hesitancy to give and to sacrifice for others has more to do with their fear of what tomorrow might bring in their own lives, than simply a lack of faith. It is about their security. Ms. Hattie's story is remarkable in part because she had so little and was willing to "sacrifice" it to help others. Her selflessness strikes us for its courage, generosity, and spirit. She gave so much, not knowing what tomorrow might bring for her. Her life was radical and risky. Say what we will about most of our lives, but *radical* and *risky* are usually not the first descriptors.

Now, does that mean that wealthy people don't have it or that they can't affect the work of God's kingdom? Absolutely not! There are countless stories of people with great resources who have given significantly to assist with the building of the God's kingdom, and their gifts are tremendous. The question is, do they give *all* of what they have? Or is there enough left over at the end of the day, and plenty of resources, to guide and watch over their family? I am not saying that wealthy people and their gifts are not needed and that they are not remarkable. When Jesus told the story of a widow who made an offering (see Mark 12:41-44; Luke 21:1-4), he emphasized the fact that she gave "out of her poverty" rather than her wealth, of which she had none. As Jesus points out, there is a difference in giving out of our poverty and giving out of our abundance. It is a powerful nuance that teaches us about the importance of real sacrifice.

My wife and I have wonderful salaries and a great life for our family. We have never gone without enough food or without enough money to buy nice clothes or to live in a nice house. No one would accuse us of living out of our poverty. I am sure that many of you are the same.

Some of you are going to read this section and recoil: "I can't give like Ms. Hattie, and I certainly can't give like the widow." No, probably not. Well, let me rephrase that . . . yes, we could. But not all of us have been given the spiritual gift of giving, and not all of us are able to throw caution to the wind. At least, not yet. Besides, nowhere in the Bible does Christ equate the amount of resources we can give away, either in their abundance or their poverty, with the amount of our faith. But, the Bible does equate the willingness of our hearts to participate from the soul-side out as the measure for how God sees our faithfulness in what we confess, and how others see our faithfulness in what we proclaim. When Jesus encountered a rich, young ruler and instructed him to sell all that he owned and give the money to the poor (see Matthew 19:16-30; Mark 10:17-31; Luke 18:18-30), it wasn't the money that the rich, young ruler struggled with. It was what was at the center of his soul, what he was really willing to sacrifice. For many people, money is not tops on this list. Countless other things rank as more valuable. But, all of us are called to respond and to do so with the full measure of all that we have.

Let me pause and add that I am not saying that if we don't have the spiritual gift of giving that we are somehow given a pass for sharing our resources. Any Christian should realize how unreasonable that view is and how self-centered that position becomes. No, we may not possess every spiritual gift but we *do* respect every gift and participate in each gift to the level that it is possible and acceptable in God's will. For instance, the Bible does not command all of us to speak in tongues, so that gift is more directed and specific to those who exercise that gift along with the gift of interpretation of tongues. But the Bible does command that we give a tithe of the firstfruits from the storehouse, and so all of us participate in that gift because of that command and because of God's will.

Those who have the spiritual gift of giving participate in that command but also in the further education, support, encouragement, broadening, and framing of how "giving" represents God's ultimate plan and gift in Jesus, and how that plan comes to life in each of us. Remember, you can't do EVERYthing. Not everyone is called to give all of his or her resources away or to make that decision. When it comes to the SOMEthing that God has planted in your heart and in your life, you will be called to give *all*—all of your life, all of your skills, and all of your resources to live out that calling. You will be called to sacrifice. It is like a beautiful puzzle with many pieces fitted together to make one image. Sure, other pieces can be fit into place, but they will never look as the original had intended.

As Paul describes, sacrifice is not just about God gathering in the resources for what it takes to accomplish the task, it is about freeing you up to the point where God can work in your heart and mind—repositioning you in order to provide God's will for your life and the direction for your next steps.

When I think about it that way, I have run into a *lot* of Ms. Hatties, people who are willing to give their all in order to accomplish what God has placed in front of them. That giving, that sacrifice, is not always profound. It doesn't have to be. It is, however, always within God's greater work and God's desire for how we make a difference in the world.

The concept of *sacrifice* is where we focus on what God wants for our lives and not on what we want. We have to be willing either to give up or to take on the things or people necessary to make it work. This is a common refrain in Scripture. If you look at the stories of Noah, Moses, Elijah, Jeremiah, Ruth, Jonah, Peter, Mary (that one . . . and yes, that one, too), James and John, or Timothy, you will see very different people with one powerful principle in common: when God asked them to give up everything, they did just that, and they followed God. They didn't all do it the same way. Some whined, some doubted, some griped, and some ran and hid, while still others simply quickly fell in line. Truthfully, they all, in the end, sacrificed the one thing that they were most scared of letting go, namely their own skills and strength. Yet look what happened through their witness and their stories.

There is a price to this kind of sacrifice, though, and we will talk about it in the next chapter. This kind of sacrifice requires *obedience*. The other part of each of the stories mentioned above is that those who are remembered for doing their SOMEthings stayed the course and played their scenario out to the end.

I once left a ministry situation where I had wanted to leave many times before I actually made the decision to depart. In fact, I had asked in a hundred different ways for God to let me off the hook, but God wouldn't. However, looking back now, I realize that the situation was really about how and when God needed me to serve and to be faithful. My sacrifice to follow God's will in that season of my life not only got the job done, it worked something new inside of me, taught me a new lesson, and reshaped a little part of my heart and soul for the next adventure.

Keep in mind that you have to be willing to put down certain things in order to take up other things. What are you willing to put down? What are you ready to sacrifice in order to accomplish your SOMEthing for God? These are important questions. These questions are the proverbial line in the sand, the demarcation between those who talk about serving God and those who get the dirt of life under their fingernails from scratching and working hard for God to make it all happen.

Remember, too, that God's way, the way of sacrifice, is not easy; you'll have to give up on the idea that it can or will be. You can't move ahead thinking that you can balance your comfort with God's plan. Frankly, when we hold to such thinking, God has better things to do. So do you.

CHAPTER 7
We Must Be *Obedient*

James 4:6-10

My Help Comes from the Left

At first glance, my neighbor is quiet and unassuming. To many, he is another staff member at a local church, a dedicated servant who remains behind the scenes while others receive the glory. However, there is more than meets the eye with this faithful brother in Christ. He doesn't just talk about loving Jesus; he shows it with every aspect of his heart and life. An engineer with an MBA, my neighbor left his job of eighteen years to enter local-church ministry as the business administrator for a local Baptist church. A couple of years later, he founded a mission ministry that uses recreation with children in under-resourced areas from the Ninth Ward of New Orleans to the slums of Costa Rica. To many of us, my neighbor is a modern-day saint who embodies the best of what the "hands and feet of the gospel" can be. His witness is faithful, as he uses his administrative skills to guide and build teams that make a difference in their communities and well beyond.

My neighbor is the man I consider "my" pastor. A few years ago when I had open-heart surgery, he visited me every day for weeks, and he sent Scripture passages to me via text messages as a reminder of God's presence. Each passage perfectly focused on my struggle or concern for that particular day. When it was time for me to take my first post-surgery steps around the hospital, the Scripture he sent from Isaiah said that I would "mount up with wings like eagles," that I would walk and "not be weary" (Isaiah

40:31 NKJV). A few days later, when I was tired and worried about what tomorrow might bring, I received a beautiful Scripture passage from him about finding courage and not being afraid. He ministered better than any ordained pastor I know. It is part of his calling, one of the many gifts that God has given him.

When I think of my neighbor, I remember the words of Psalm 121:1: "I will lift up my eyes to the hills—From whence comes my help?" (NKJV). In a world that struggles to find its voice and its connection to God, he simply listens to the echo of God's spirit, and he then goes into the world and lives like Jesus. He is obedient in where God leads him and faithful to follow God's plan for his life. For those of us whose heart he touches with his gentle obedience to God's Word, we need not look as far as the hills for help. In fact, I just go to my front porch and look left.

Draw Near to God

In the biblical book named for him, James says, "Draw near to God, and he will draw near to you . . ." (4:8). This verse is largely misread as an ultimatum from God. But nothing could be further from the truth. Instead, the Scripture offers some commonsense wisdom. How do you embrace someone who refuses to open his or her arms? How can you look deeply into someone's eyes when that person refuses to make eye contact? How do you truly know someone who refuses to let you into his or her heart and life? Scripture tells us that God is always near. God is not the problem. The real question is whether we will draw near to God.

To accomplish the SOMEthing God has in store for our lives, we must follow where God leads, even when the situation is uncomfortable and difficult. Obedience leads us beyond what we can see or understand. Obedience happens when we commit ourselves to a closer walk with God. Obedience is not meant to be hard or difficult. In fact, it should be an outflow of what God has planted inside of us. The challenge in obedience lies in being able to wade past the world's other requirements and in redefining the nature of how we are called to make a difference. We usually have set up our lives with so many people we have to please before we feel comfortable letting go and letting God work, that we substitute worrying about the feelings of others for how we should live obedient lives for God. Thus, for so many of us, working for our SOMEthing that God has planted in each of us becomes just another task, another struggle, and we miss the joy God has in store for us. We are so busy trying to make everyone else happy that we forget the One we should and must make happy if we are to discover what our purpose in God might mean for the world, and how it can change our communities.

That's right, God is looking to us to change our communities, and that happens when we obey what, how, and where God is planting that mission inside of us, not how we are to keep the plates spinning or the balls in the air, or how many people we can keep from getting mad at us, or how many of our to-do list tasks we check off. No, God wants us to listen, follow, and change.

The passage from James provides some great practical principles for how we respond to God's call in our lives:

> He gives us more grace. That is why Scripture says:
> "God opposes the proud
> but gives grace to the humble."
> Submit yourselves, then, to God. Resist the devil, and he will flee from you. Come near to God and he will come near to you. Wash your hands, you sinners, and purify your hearts, you double-minded. Grieve, mourn and wail. Change your laughter to mourning and your joy to gloom. Humble yourselves before the Lord, and he will lift you up. (4:6-10 NIV)

First, James tells us, we are to live *humble* lives. The first act of obedience is not about following the rules as much as it's about becoming humble and thankful before the Lord. This sounds like really flowery language, I know, but James is clear that what can only be interpreted as pride pushes God away while it is humility that draws God to us. The practical reason for this, Scripture says, is that when we confront prideful people in our lives, we can only confront them with humility. It is hard to tell persons who already believe they know everything something that might help them grow; but we can show them the other side, provide another picture for how the scenario might look.

Second, according to James we are to "submit" ourselves to God. In verse 7, James says this must be a specific act of worship because as we are working our way toward God, the Adversary is working to pull us from God and distract us from where God wants us to be in our lives. This spiritual act of worship is humbling and obedient. Once we make a "habit" of this kind of life, the Adversary flees from us or, as I like to put it, just gets tired of trying.

Third, we are then able to draw close to God and discover the full portion of what God has in store for us. We will discover that God's plan in our lives is not only for us to do SOMEthing significant for the Kingdom; it is for our own good and is filled with joy. Why joy? Because as we draw close to God, God draws close to us and fulfills in us God's long-awaited plan, created just for us as a fulfillment of the relationship. What a beautiful way to look at it! Obedience is the bridge back to *what* and *who* God wanted to be in us all along.

Remember, obedience is not just about following the rules. So many have interpreted obedience as "getting in line" or "staying in order." That is only the first and one small part of our relationship with God. I don't like that characterization of obedience anyway because it demeans the relational nature of God's incredible love for us. Instead, the goal of obedience, as I mentioned earlier, is that we might know the full measure of what God is doing in our lives; then, as we go forward to live it out, we might have a blast as we watch the wonderful ways it comes to fruition in and through us. Remember, it is God's prerogative, will, and expectation, James says, to draw close to us. Can you imagine anything more worthy of our obedience? Frankly, my friend, I don't want to miss that. I don't want you to miss it either. God drawing close to us is the extravagant act of the God of the Universe to be in the "midst of us" and to love us unconditionally while there. Through obedience, that is what God did for my neighbor, and it is what God will do for us as well.

CHAPTER 8

We Must Grow to *Maturity*

1 Thessalonians 3:8-13

A Boy Named Ryan

In 2007, I had the privilege of sharing keynote responsibilities at a World AIDS Day event with Jeanne White, mother of AIDS activist and victim Ryan White. Ryan was born a few months after me. He died at the age of eighteen after a hard and much-publicized battle with the disease. He had been prevented from registering for school in the Indiana town where he grew up in the 1980s. The news outlets jumped at the chance to chronicle the fight, which, at the time, was only one of the public struggles throughout the country over the rights of AIDS victims and of hemophiliacs. The story drew a great deal of attention and made Ryan an instant celebrity. It also brought him new friends in such noted public figures as Elton John, Michael Jackson, and Elizabeth Taylor.

More than this celebrity, though, Ryan fought a valiant fight and became an example to everyone in the battle and all those living with the disease. His life served as an example to all of us. Ryan, though just a young boy when he began his fight against AIDS, not only carried himself with dignity, he also became a role model for how to deal with difficult choices and places in our lives. People were amazed that this young teenage boy could show such maturity, strength, and courage in the face of such opposition—opposition both from the disease and from others.

Although our paths never crossed, being so close in age I felt as though I knew Ryan; everyone fighting AIDS or close to the issue in some way felt as though they knew him. As Ryan fought his battle with HIV in the public eye, I, like many others, fought the battle privately. I remember watching Ryan's very public battle and wondering what the strain of the limelight meant for him. I would learn later that Ryan had the same aspirations, fears, and challenges as other boys our age. It was just that his story played out on television screens and through the lens of a camera.

That night in 2007 at the World AIDS Day conference, Ryan White's mother, Jeanne, and I spent time talking about those days before the world "got on board" in the fight against AIDS and before the host of medicines used to treat people and to save lives were available. Those were difficult times that possessed few redeeming factors except that a few people courageously came forward to stand up for those whom the Scriptures would refer to as "the least of these."

Jeanne told Ryan's story of rejection and discrimination as he revealed his disease. He was a champion in the fight at a time when AIDS was a death sentence and when disclosing one's condition did not elicit sympathy as much as suspicion, fear, and prejudice. There were no medical treatments, and little was known of the disease. Ryan stepped into the storm with bravery and maturity that astounded all those who watched. His life became a symbol of courage and strength that inspired a nation, and he paved the way for so many of us with the disease.

Following the conference, Jeanne White told me that Ryan would have liked my life. It was a beautiful comment for me to hear. I had wondered if she had made a connection between my age and Ryan's. As I had told my story, I had looked over at her several times and could sense that she was framing my narrative within the narrative of her own son, who had not been as fortunate. We talked for a minute about Ryan's dreams and aspirations, and about those final months when he struggled to live as normal a life as possible, all the while suspecting that his body could not go much further.

She reminded all of us standing there what a witness Ryan was, especially at that time of the disease. He showed us things about AIDS, and life for that matter, that we could not have learned on our own.

I wish I could have known him.

I realized that sometimes in life, circumstances allow us easier roads. Other times, we grow up fast, much too fast for any child. Maturity comes with meaning, and when life requires the unthinkable from us, our strength to cope and even prevail is not as far away as we might first imagine. Ryan was mature beyond his years, but not just in his attitude. His spirit and soul spoke to something rooted firmly in faith, and not just faith in God. Ryan had a faith in others that saw beyond our frail and fragile imperfections. Ironically, the more he struggled, the more he grew. The more he grew, the more he understood. The more he understood, the clearer he saw others—almost the way God sees us.

Our level of maturity, in large part, defines our ability to move forward not only in what God has given us to accomplish, but also in how we face the difficulties along the way. Whereas *sacrifice* is the launching pad for our SOMEthing, and *obedience* is the engine, *maturity* is our compass for shaping our direction and destination.

Holy Confidence

> For now we really live, since you are standing firm in the Lord. How can we thank God enough for you in return for all the joy we have in the presence of our God because of you? Night and day we pray most earnestly that we may see you again and supply what is lacking in your faith.
>
> Now may our God and Father himself and our Lord Jesus clear the way for us to come to you. May the Lord make your love increase and overflow for each other and for everyone else, just as ours does for you. May he strengthen your hearts so that you will be blameless and holy in the presence of our God and Father when our Lord Jesus comes with all his holy ones. (1 Thessalonians 3:8-13 NIV)

When the Apostle Paul wrote the letter to the church in Thessalonica, he wanted to encourage them to continue what God had started in their fellowship. There was much to do, and Paul had walked them through several instructions for not only finding perseverance in difficult times, but also for maturing in their faith so that they would become all that God had planned for them. Stopping short was not enough for God, and Paul wanted the folks at Thessalonica to know that.

As Paul saw, most of the followers' struggles were a result not of their inability to stand firm, but their inability to grow from their times of struggle. In his second letter to the church at Thessalonica, Paul tells them to "stand firm" in their struggles and to hold fast to what he had taught them (2 Thessalonians 2:13-15). This wasn't so that they would remain in the same spiritual place, but so that they would, over the course of their relationships in Christ, grow deeper in their faith. Later in this same letter, Paul raises the bar again by saying that he has "confidence in the Lord" that the good people of Thessalonica not only were persevering but were prevailing and growing stronger in their understanding (2 Thessalonians 3:4). It is such a concern for Paul that they continue to strengthen their faith that he spends several verses warning them against idleness (2 Thessalonians 3:6-13). Idleness leads to all sorts of other struggles, Paul insists, with the most severe being a spiritual apathy.

Growing deeper—gaining maturity—provides the roots by which obedience becomes a way of life. Faith, much like a tree, grows up and out in relation to how deeply it has planted its roots. Another aspect of this in Scripture is when Paul says that not only does God expect us to grow deeper, God desires maturity for us. God opens his heart that we might be in relationship, and God unveils the deep riches of what that relationship can become.

As we grow deeper in our relationship with God, our gifts become more vital. The more vital our gifts, the more God works in and through our lives, using our resources to do significant things. Growing deeper in our walk with God is not easy. As with so many things, anything worth having and keeping or maintaining at a certain level will require a lot of hard work. Maturity is no different. For it to grow, it will take effort.

Old but Not Mature

For us to accomplish our SOMEthing in Christ, we will have to leave our old habits and understandings behind. It is that simple. It will also require, as the Scripture says, that we "renew" our minds and stretch our intellect. This process expands our understanding, certainly, but it also provides a "spiritual structure" for how we process what God calls us to be and do. Knowing God's word better and understanding the riches of God's presence through Christ and the Holy Spirit are important. And, thus, accomplishing our SOMEthing requires a maturing of our understanding of God's work in and through us.

God also requires that we grow in our ability to love one another and to be in ministry and fellowship with one another. As I mentioned earlier, maturity is not just about the ways we process information and respond, but also about how we process relationships and situations and then formulate solutions for moving forward in life's circumstances. In neither case does age or position have anything to do with the depth of a person or a group of people. Instead, it is really their spiritual maturity level that makes the most difference in them.

Recently I worked with a congregation that is nearly sixty years old. They have accomplished much in their history together and have lots of achievements to show for it and to be proud of. However, with all they have accomplished, I discovered their spiritual acumen is not mature. Not even close. How do I know this? Well, I was introduced to the congregation with the express purpose of assisting them in changing the worship service, to make a transition to a different style of worship. A small, committed group of people both approved and supported this process wholeheartedly. But, as the plan unfolded, those who had not been part of the leadership's discussions pushed back harshly, reacting in some ways that led others to say they "did not recognize their own church." Clearly, the hot-button issue of worship change unveiled a level of uncertainty, mistrust, and long-buried issues with which the congregation was unprepared to deal. And, thus, as has happened countless times through the history of the Body of Christ, very good people responded in very negative, un-Christlike ways.

Not only were they unable to transition the service, but they also fundamentally could not facilitate the conversations needed to begin the process in the first place. They had grown very good at maintaining a system of growth that required only surface responses to relationships, programs, staff, worship, and so on. But they couldn't go deeper. They didn't have the maturity, no matter how much growth they had experienced.

The result was that this congregation had been very successful in growing the congregation "wider" but they had not grown very deep. The one thing they needed most to achieve the "next level" was the one thing they had sacrificed in order to "be all things to all people." Beyond that, they could not go any further. The pastor asked me what I thought could be done. It was not a simple answer. The same philosophies that had led to numerical growth would not work in "righting the ship" and providing for a new, better direction. We would need to begin at the basics. I suggested four parts to the solution.

First, the congregation needed to learn their Bibles. They had formulated truth by taking "snippets" of Scripture and then using those to foster enough conversation or momentum for the task at hand. Real growth demanded real connection to God's word. It is the same for our maturity. We cannot grow past what we know of God's word.

Second, the congregation needed a spiritual formation plan that began with growing smaller before they grew larger. In one survey, one church that had an average worship attendance of nearly 1,500 people admitted to having only about 6 percent of their members in ongoing, long-term connections. Quite simply, the members of that church didn't know each other. Biblical community is one of the best ways Christ himself uses to help his followers grow deeper.

Third, the congregation needed to serve in ways that pushed them way beyond their boundaries and comfort zones. They could not see that their deeply ingrained programs were self-serving, that they were dealing primarily with the needs present within their own congregation. The real spiritual maturity was taking place among this church's youth and children, who were "getting their hands and feet dirty" for God. But the youth and children of this church possessed no power or authority for modeling this concept, and they usually were relegated to a backseat position for being examples. The result was a congregation that served as it seemed comfortable—and they were *very* comfortable.

Fourth and finally, this congregation needed "holy, sacred moments" that pricked their souls and changed their lives. They had come to expect certain things from church, and church never disappointed them; but they also never asked the church to "jump very high," either. In doing so, they missed the moments of awe and wonder that become the sail winds for how churches move forward. Without them, the church will die because it stops growing.

The pastor of this church tried using several of these suggestions and noted a tremendous amount of success among those who took on the challenge. "The problem," he said, "is that a new group of mature believers has risen up with a new set of expectations, creating a real struggle with our church's power structures."

"How have the current power structures responded?" I asked.

"Not very well," he replied. "They see these new folks as 'upstarts' who have not 'paid their dues.'"

"How do the new folks respond?" I asked.

The pastor thought about it for a while, and then said with a smile, "They really don't care."

"And they won't," I said. This is because they have moved beyond the old way of seeing and doing church. It doesn't mean the conflict is over. Most likely it is only just beginning. But it means that the ground rules have changed. Those in this congregation who really desire spiritual growth will need to get behind their spiritually mature leaders and pray for them and support them. And, yes, together they can take the hill, as long as they believe it is worth it.

Maturity changes not only how we see God and ourselves, but also how we see our potential for responding to God's challenge in our lives, both as individuals and as communities. It changes how we see others. Spiritual maturity should not be a form of snobbery, but it certainly involves a holy discontent that has little patience for those who hold to the status quo and see no room for change or growth.

It is just that when we see that deeper glimpse of God and what God's purpose for us is, the old issues, the old ways, seem so unimportant. That is what the Apostle Paul meant when he said, "Be transformed by the renewing of your minds" (Romans 12:2), not that we would start to think like others, but that we would start to think like God. This will not only change your world and your church, it also will change *you* and push you one step closer to finding and doing the SOMEthing God has had in store for you all along. Without it, though, we have little chance of making the kind of difference that we seek and, most importantly, that God seeks in and through us.

CHAPTER 9

We Must Model *Encouragement* and Put Forth *Effort*

Philippians 3:12-14

Like the Wind

One of the most exciting opportunities of my life was seeing the Kenyan long-distance track team in person. It was 1993 at the National Cherry Blossom Festival and race in Washington, D.C. My wife and I were attending the festival for the express purpose of seeing this unbelievable team of long-distance runners. My wife is a runner; I am not. You don't need to be a runner, though, in order to appreciate the incredible skill of these athletes, who do what they do with what appears to be very little effort. My wife and I had first discovered the Kenyan team through a friend who is an avid runner and who quickly educated us on the best in the sport. And, certainly, the Kenyan team was, at the time, the best. By the time my wife and I saw them in Washington, the Kenyan team was already the stuff of legend. Their tenacity, speed, and dominance propelled them above their competitors. The fact that many of them ran in bare feet only increased their aura.

To watch them run was more art than athleticism. They approached their sport with the same fervor and dedication as other athletes, but there was also something spiritual about their gifts. As we watched them go by, one observer standing next to me said it was as if they had been "born for this very purpose." I understood what he was saying. There is a flow to our lives, whether in athletic, intellectual, or relational pursuits, where the fit between who we are and who God has wired us up to be seems almost perfect. And it is palpable, visual, and personal. People can see it in action.

I have witnessed people at church who may not appear to have any real significance as judged by the world's standards; but offer them a chance to greet or to share their gift of hospitality, and you would consider them to be the Kenyan team, the elite talent, in terms of welcoming people. The same can be said of people who have the gift of music or working with children or praying or taking care of others. These gifts won't necessarily get you on the cover of *Sports Illustrated* or *Time*, but they will be indelible and will touch deep into peoples' lives.

And, yet, there is more to it than just doing a task or exercising a skill. The Kenyan team ran with passion as though they carried not just their own hopes and dreams, but also the aspirations of everyone from their country. They ran with spirit and focus and technical perfection to the point that the marathons they ran appeared much easier to accomplish than they really were. And, in the process, the Kenyan team redefined the sport. They ran because, as they would later note, they loved it and it was who they were as though—yes, wait for it—they had been "born for this task." Who is to say they were not. This was their gift, and they lived it out with passion.

Research deeper into their habits and history, and you will see that this team's success began at the same place as all successful endeavors: effort. These runners didn't just live off of passion; no one can do that. No, they channeled their love of their sport into incredible effort, practice, and hard work. They knew their passion and gifts had given them an edge, but they also knew that to accomplish being the best at what they loved so much would require them to work hard and to be more focused than anyone else.

A View of Such Things

Not that I have already obtained all this, or have already been made perfect, but I press on to take hold of that for which Christ Jesus took hold of me. Brothers, I do not consider myself yet to have taken hold of it. But one thing I do: Forgetting what is behind and straining toward what is ahead, I press on toward the goal to win the prize for which God has called me heavenward in Christ Jesus.

All of us who are mature should take such a view of things. (Philippians 3:12-15a NIV)

The Apostle Paul's words to the church at Philippi are about gratitude, hard work, and living up to our potential. They are also about effort and keeping focused on the good work that God has placed in our lives.

Look at the passage above. No one loves Paul more than these people, and vice versa. Part of their relationship is about encouraging one another, but in a different way from, say, how Paul encouraged the Corinthians. Paul sees the Christian believers of Philippi as possessing incredible potential that is natural and important to the body of Christ, and he does not want them to miss that fact.

Paul is also "running a race" to live out what God has gifted inside of him (see 1 Corinthians 9:24-25). It is easy for us to look at the life of Paul and forget that he was not gifted with EVERYthing. Indeed, he was given a very special SOMEthing that God intended for him to complete. And, yes, Paul characterized it as a race, and he knew it was his job to run it to the best of his ability and to win it. This would require of Paul the giving of his best, sacrificing, being obedient, and living a mature life. But, as Paul says to the Philippians, all of this will get you only so far. "All of us who are mature," he says, will have to go the extra mile. They will have to put forth incredible effort.

Not once but twice, Paul gives the image of "straining" and effort to do the SOMEthing that God had placed in his life. He "presses on" (Philippians 3:12), and says that he is "straining toward what is ahead" (3:13 NIV). Then, almost as if to reiterate the cheer, Paul says again, "I press on toward the goal to win the prize" (3:14 NIV). How important is this part of the process for Paul? Look at the last verse in this passage: "All of us who are mature should take such a view of things" (3:15 NIV). Quite simply, being mature means putting forth the full measure of our effort and skills. If we don't put forth that effort, Paul says, then we are not as mature as we had thought.

This is not just a spiritual pep talk. These are Paul's words to people he loves, about the work given to him by the God he loves.

This is a heart-to-heart message; Paul does not want to miss the "prize" in his life, and he doesn't want anyone else to miss the prize in their lives either.

Moving Mountains

Several years ago, I had the privilege of becoming friends with the head coach of an NCAA Division I football team. The team was well disciplined and well managed, and my friend had a decade-and-a-half streak of winning seasons. He knew how to get the most out of his players, and he knew that first and foremost, even before a single pass was thrown or one play called, discipline and commitment in the weight room were critical. I had the chance to speak to the team before a game one night and also to spend some time with some of the players, a group of young men who were incredibly hard-working, polite, and focused.

Occasionally I would take my daughters with me to the field house to watch the players at work in the weight rooms. There were restrictions on where we could stand, but we spent a lot of time watching these enormous men lift weights that oftentimes weighed twice as much as I did, and more. We watched as the team members gave their all with such intensity. They lifted with passion and purpose, and one could see that they were doing more than "getting in shape"; they were preparing for battle.

One of our favorite parts of the visit was to watch the deadlift portions of the weight lifting schedule. This is where, from a standing position, the men would lift enormous amounts of weight. It was a resistance training drill of the highest order, meant to create huge amounts of muscle. My daughters were amazed at how much weight the players lifted, and they wanted to know why they went through a drill that seemed so different from what the players actually would be doing on the field. I explained that muscle is developed by lifting and being tested with large amounts of resistance. The more resistance, the more muscle their body would build. Their effort, though painful and difficult, would eventually make them stronger and able to handle more weight and resistance on the football field.

After watching them for a few minutes, my middle daughter said, "It is like watching 'moving mountains.'" That phrase, "moving mountains," could mean one of two things. Watching the players' activity was very much like seeing huge "mountains of men" moving, lumbering through the weight room. But, it also illustrates the same process God gives to us, to you and me, in order to move the mountains of our lives. Yet, oftentimes, it takes facing our resistance in order to grow strong enough to get the job done.

You *have not*, because you have not put forth the effort to ask—to be stronger—to be better. Effort is an incredible "line in the sand" between those who "get by," and those who "prevail" and "exceed" at levels once thought unimaginable.

A couple of years ago, this same coaching friend of mine was let go from his position as head football coach at this school. He had continued to produce winning teams, but the school's administration questioned whether the program was making the right improvements and great enough strides in terms of going to the next level of competition. For me, on a personal level, his dismissal was difficult. I knew the kind of man my friend was, how much he loved the kids, and how much he did for the community. I did not take his firing very well.

A couple of weeks after everything had died down, another friend who was close to both of us said that it was "possibly time" for this transition—not because our friend was no longer a great coach; on the contrary, he could still win football games with the best of them. It was time, this friend said, because he had "lost the fire," and the team felt it. It was hard to admit, but I too could see what many were talking about. For my friend to take himself and his teams to that next level, it would require more than "dotting the i's" and "crossing the t's." It would require unbelievable effort and intensity against the resistance of our lives, such that it could "move mountains" if necessary.

In weight lifting and in coaching, just as in finding and accomplishing your SOMEthing in God's work, effort matters.

CHAPTER 10

One Deep Breath Before Reaching Our Potential

Before we go any further, let me say that God is ready to push you to the next level. God wants nothing more than for you to take that leap and to run the race. As you have read these previous pages, you, too, may be ready, wanting nothing more than to take the next hill and see the victory that God has planted inside of your soul. That, my friend, is what I believe God wants for you. Yet, I need to say this: not everyone is ready for the long marathon or the great race or the next hill or the grand resistance that inevitably will come your way. What we need to make sure of is that we are ready, with our feet firmly planted and our hearts ready before God. Then we can "deadlift the weight," accomplish the mission, that God has put in front of us. Otherwise, I fear we might do more harm than good.

When my family and I accepted the appointment to serve at one of the largest United Methodist churches in the country, it was both an honor and a daunting task. I had led a television ministry over the past few years and worked as a church consultant starting new congregations for nearly ten years before that. The congregation to which I now had been appointed was over fifty years old, had lived pretty much within the same paradigm for ten or more years, and had, over the last decade and a half, encountered several major issues, any one of which, by itself, would have scarred the congregation for years to come. But this congregation had dealt with no fewer than seven congregation-changing events. Added to this, in the previous five years before my arrival there had been nine senior pastor and associate pastor changeovers.

Still, the congregation had remained strong in worship attendance, averaging 2,500 on Sunday mornings, and also had
remained very active in the life of the community. The congregation was still growing, requiring a number of changes in order to
handle increased parking and overflow issues. On the surface, this
congregation presented a picture of a vibrant, innovative congregation ready for anything and everything.

As I would soon discover, however, nothing could be further
from the truth. The congregation was still hurting from violations
of trust that went back nearly fifteen years. It had not properly
grieved and healed from a host of major changes that included an
instance of immorality on the part of a senior leader, near financial
collapse, and an increasing gulf between the leadership and the
people of its two primary campuses. It was also in part an aging
congregation, with the members of one of its campuses quite resist-
ant to any of the sorts of changes needed to reach younger, more
diverse people. Now, let me say that these were and are wonderful
people. However, they had lived achieving their SOMEthing for
several generations, yet never really digging deep to ask God what
might be the next level of the plan for their church's life.

My arrival was less than auspicious. Within the first few months,
my tires were slashed, and a host of other "events" took place that
made my family question whether we had made the right choice.
Because we had been told and convinced by a long-range visioning
team plan that the congregation was ready for some changes and
transitions, we had jumped headlong into implementing several
plans for new worship services, staff redesigns, and other avenues
for accomplishing what we thought was God's plan for us. We
were wrong. The congregation experienced an immediate
pushback, with a drop in attendance and a host of disgruntled
conversations.

Eventually I pulled back on our plans, threw out the visioning
team's report, and began simply listening to what people were saying. The results were telling. I discovered a congregation more than
willing to make a difference but whose members, themselves, had
received very little in spiritual formation due to the various
changes and upheavals over the past few years. They had spent a
great deal of time in crisis mode, dealing with one urgent situation
after another, and it had become very difficult for them to accom-

plish their SOMEthing for God while running a race that wasn't for the prize, but rather for survival.

At first, I could not understand why the congregation was not ready to go to the next level, to sacrifice and to listen to what God was saying was their forward movement, until I understood that *timing, fundamentals, and a commitment to the basics* were crucial for us in order to become all that God intended for us to be and in order to reach our potential.

So, stepping back to evaluate our place and purpose going forward, before we jumped off into the deep end of the pool to reach the next level, we had to decide to ground ourselves with a few fundamental principles that would become our foundation for reaching beyond the horizon and for becoming the SOMEthing God had in store for our particular congregation.

We created a campaign, a focus for our work and our ministry that we called "Loving Jesus . . . Loving like Jesus." The basic philosophy is that it is not enough for us simply to know Jesus, to love Jesus, or to want to follow Jesus. *We must want to love like Jesus in the world if we are to be successful.* In this focus, we drew inspiration from several Bible passages to remind us of God's great love and God's expectations for us, but finally we settled on Acts 2:42-47 as the model for our daily walk and commitment so in EVERY way we can be ready for where God sends us. In focusing on this passage of Scripture and on these first believers, we learned the principles God required from the beginning, knowing that God, whose message remains unchanged, would still require them of us today. Here are those principles.

First, *God requires us to study our Bibles and to know his Word.* Nothing substitutes for knowing God's word, written and on the page, but also God's Word (with a capital "W") and seeing where the life of Christ instructs, encourages, and guides us today.

Second, *God requires us to live in community and to do life together.* One of the most important lessons for accomplishing our SOMEthing is that God never intended for us to accomplish it alone.

Third, *God requires us to share our resources.* We may never have enough, but we still are held in account to give from both our abundance and our poverty, to share without question, and to be consistent and generous. The way we manage and share our resources is a tangible marker for the progress we are making in accomplishing our SOMEthing for God.

Fourth, *God requires us to serve faithfully*—not just in terms of accomplishing our SOMEthing, but in taking on a servant's heart. We must model kindness, love, peace, joy, and self-control for our families, friends, and loved ones. This model, more than anything, redirects our potential in building community and in refreshing our own interests and relationships in accomplishing—yes—our SOMEthing for God.

Fifth, *God requires us to worship boldly.* A friend of mine likes to say, "No matter what, always worship like you mean it." This, more than anything, changes the dynamics of our life with God. Being in his presence causes a reaction that forces a response. It is awesome, frightening, energizing, refreshing, powerful, personal, poignant . . . it is worship. Enjoy it.

Once we instituted this time and study in our church's life, much changed. The anxiety of the past and the fear of the future subsided, not completely, but enough for us to really "see" each other and go forward. And people began to trust one another again. People began to see church as more than another institution from whom and for whom much is expected. Instead, they began to see faith as a relationship, and they were ready to know more. If your church or fellowship is not ready for this, don't fret; maybe that is your SOMEthing at this point, to help them take steps needed for growth and for reaching their potential. Also, don't let it distract you from recognizing God's work in your life. If your church or fellowship group is struggling as mine was, realize that these struggles are not equivalent to your ability to accomplish what God has wired up in your spiritual DNA. *The church* is an institution; you are in relationship with the living God of the universe. Yes, there is a difference.

So why am I telling you this now? We have discussed in this book how God has wired each of us and gifted us with SOMEthing to accomplish for him. We know that we can't do EVERYthing, and that part of the joy of who we are in Christ is being in relationship with our brothers and sisters in the faith. Not all churches and Christ followers (your brothers and sisters) are at the same place, and you may experience some resistance as you move forward in deepening your faith and your service for Christ. Let me rephrase that: you most certainly *will* experience resistance, but don't fret or become worried. First of all, God is more than aware of your situation and what is happening in your church or faith fellowship; and although you are called to assist in the life of your congregation, it is not your job to fix your church's problems. In this, too, we can't do EVERYthing.

We can, however, do SOMEthing to help our church be healthier. Here are a few suggestions: Pray for the church. Encourage your brothers and sisters. Support your pastor. Be faithful in living out your covenant commitments in attending church, sharing your gifts, and offering your service.

All the while, keep in mind the principles outlined above as markers for your congregation's health and for how much time and effort you might expend in helping your local church become what God needs it to be. I believe this will help in two ways. First, it will always serve as a point of reference for what a healthy church looks like, keeping to a minimum the distractions from things that ultimately are not important. Second, it will remind each of us that what we have to accomplish in Christ is bigger than even our local fellowship and the petty designs we often develop in our local churches.

Remember, God's plan is to amaze you with the simplicity and power of what your SOMEthing is meant to accomplish for the whole Body. That does not mean that everyone is going to get it or like it. But, it does mean that God is going to show up, and, my friend, that is more than enough.

So, sermon over. And, like many of our churches should do, let's get back to becoming what God has in store for us. For there is the real point, the real purpose.

PART III

"ANYthing Is Possible"

It may sound overly simple. But when we realize that we cannot achieve EVERYthing, but that God has given to each of us a SOMEthing that we are to accomplish in God, the potential of the body of Christ becomes clear. Throughout the New Testament, the Apostle Paul discusses the importance of spiritual gifts. In doing so, he makes three important claims that define the impact of what the body of Christ can and should become. First, God has given everyone a passion area, and to every believer God has given a spiritual gift that, through the power of the Holy Spirit, God intends for us to use in service for building the Kingdom. Second, no one person has every gift; but in every situation, God raises up those gifts that are necessary for accomplishing the goals of the Kingdom. Third and finally, God intends for each of us to use our gift in whatever way, place, or season God has planted within us. If we do not use our gift for God's purpose, God will bring forth others who will fill in the gaps, but the gift God has given us, *our* gift, will never be used the way God intended unless we are the ones employing it. The point, for Paul, is for everyone to use his or her spiritual gift in his or her passion area to expand God's work and will in grace and love, so that more people come into a relationship with Christ, and so that the needs of the world are met through the committed faithfulness of Christ's followers.

Which raises the question: what is the potential for the body of Christ if all of us use our spiritual gifts, if each one of us does his or her SOMEthing, to make a difference? The answer is, simply, ANYthing is possible.

Several years ago, Saddleback Community Church adopted an initiative in the nation of Rwanda that set a new course for how churches, through a variety of issues, could make a difference in Africa. What Saddleback Church realized was that whereas government and nonprofit organizations had little ability to impact the whole of oftentimes fragile nations, *churches* existed in every community and village. This became the point of mobilization, deployment, and distribution for a variety of services, including medicines, information, and education. It was brilliant, since this is what the first church understood so well itself in living and sharing the love of Christ. *None* of us is as strong as *all* of us. And the body of Christ, when truly acting like the body of Christ, is strongest of all.

Saddleback is not special in this approach; this is the *biblical* approach. In the midst of the emotion and betrayal and anger that this world so often entails, the God of the universe put together a plan: if everyone will do his or her part, then ANYthing is possible. Simple. Powerful. God.

CHAPTER 11

We Are Able to *Abound* and Live in *Abundance*

Romans 12:4-10

Sharing God

Maggie loved the story from children's church about Jesus being our "rock." The teacher had handed each child a small rock and had told the children to remember God's love for them every time they saw or touched this rock. The rock was tangible, a way for Maggie and the other children to hold on to something when thinking about God. So many times in the children's moments at her church, the leader talked about God in ways that did not put flesh on God, ways that left the children with a wonderful lesson of words but little that they could *feel* or *use*. Maggie liked this particular children's church moment, because it gave her something usable and real.

Maggie took her rock home and kept it safe on her nightstand. She would place it in her pocket for school, rarely going anywhere without it. She was old enough to know that God was not the rock, and that the rock was not God; but Maggie liked the idea of being able to reach into her pocket and touch the rock and be reminded that God was always with her.

One day, Maggie's mother saw Maggie in the back yard collecting one rock after another. Maggie was deliberate and careful, dusting off each rock as she placed it into her bag. Her mother, eager to know what she was doing, called out to Maggie from the back porch. "What are you doing, Maggie?" her mother asked.

"Picking up rocks," Maggie replied.

"What for?" her mother asked.

"I'm going to share God with my friends," Maggie quickly answered. So she did. Maggie went to school and gave rocks to her friends. When someone new came to town or joined the class, it was easy: there were plenty of rocks to go around, and it was easy to go find another one to share with whoever was new to their little community.

What Maggie knew is that with the abundance of rocks lying around her yard, how easy it was to simply pick up a new one to share. This is something that as Christians we so often forget. God is bigger than we imagine, and there is plenty to go around. God is as close as our hearts and souls and as easy to share as it was for Maggie to share that rock.

When we in the body of Christ are working together to do our SOMEthings, then ANYthing becomes possible. The first result of this is that with each of us working together, God's grace grows in its abundance and abounds in every word, deed, or action we share. And, thus, there is a limitless supply of grace that grows up in our faithful commitment to what God has called us to do.

Quite a List

The first time I really noticed the many gifts that God had given us in Scripture was when I took my first spiritual gifts inventory. I remember being excited to find out what my spiritual gifts were. When I learned that my top three gifts were faith, leadership, and teaching, they seemed to fit, as those had been the places where I had felt the most comfortable and that had provided the most excitement for me in working in the body of Christ. It seemed simple and even almost anticlimactic that God would gift me in those places where I best enjoyed working in the first place. But, that is the nature of what God's gifts for us should do—they meet us at the point of our greatest passion, interest, and abilities. Neither one is mutually exclusive.

The list of spiritual gifts mentioned in Scripture is impressive. It includes many of the more notable gifts that we normally recognize and celebrate, gifts such as teaching and preaching, singing and other creative arts, praying, and so on. In the spiritual gifts inventory I took, there were other gifts mentioned that I had not thought as much about, including hospitality, leadership, wisdom, and discernment. Yet the more I thought about the importance of each of these gifts in what I had seen of the work of the church, the more I realized the importance of the general scope it covered and how, by its very nature, it echoed what we could not do alone. And, thus, like clockwork, God has provided, in one way or another, for each of the gifts in each setting I have been a part of.

The first church I served as a pastor was small and aging, and, many believed, unable to move beyond its bounds of doing things the same old way as before. The people had been given little example to believe anything else. In one of my first acts as pastor, however, I had the church members fill out a spiritual gifts assessment. What I discovered among that group of fewer than fifty people was that God had provided, in one person or another, each of the spiritual gifts, including those more obscure ones such as prophecy and craftsmanship. Even in a small-membership church like that one, there was no shortage of spiritual gifts. And the more people took note of their gifts and then sought to live them out, the more the body of Christ became available to do God's work in places and ways that, earlier, had seemed difficult or even impossible. God's gifts were as abundant as the rocks Maggie picked up for her friends. It seemed no accident; and, of course, it wasn't.

God has provided an abundance of gifts that abound in many forms and places for the season of ministry or life in which you find yourself. When the church is working together, seeking out their SOMEthings, the body of Christ is more than able to move forward and accomplish amazing things for the Kingdom. Is it easy? No. Does everyone always comply? Of course not. Each situation is unique, but it does not negate what God has planned from the beginning. Just because we may not live it out personally or see the evidence of these gifts in those around us, it does not mean that God has not done God's part on the front end. When we as the body of Christ do our SOMEthings, we always have what we need, and what we need is sufficient.

CHAPTER 12

We Are Able to Safely *Navigate* Life's Journey

1 Corinthians 12:27

Markers for the Journey

Fred bought a new boat and invited my family for a harbor cruise. We spent the day on the water, including a trip to an island some thirty minutes offshore. It was a beautiful day, but it was also a day when we learned some lessons about boats and the sea. Some people believe that you simply put the boat into the water and go. This is a dangerous and unreasonable concept if you are trying to make a safe voyage. Of course, I must admit that I was one of those people who did not understand the importance of knowing your business while boating and understanding the critical nature of life on the water. I learned that these lessons also illustrate our work as the body of Christ on dry land.

First, when captaining the vessel and making the voyage, you must stay within the charted areas, especially around other boats and when coming close to shore. Paying attention to the nautical "markers" makes an important difference. We navigate in four critical ways: (1) First, you must have a compass that gives you your direction. In most large open areas, there is no point of reference. (2) Second, you need a directional map to pinpoint your coordinates so that you know your location as you move to your destination, through your direction. (3) Third, it helps to have a depth finder that maps out the depth of the water and shows what debris may lie under you when sailing forward. (4) Finally, you need to watch for the navigational markers as you get close to shore. These red and green markers serve as a guide for the channel not only to help boats as they work and sail together, but also to make sure that everyone stays in appropriate depth levels, not getting too close to shore and into danger.

Second, everyone on a boat plays a part, even if they are primarily sightseeing. We are all to keep our eyes out for other boats, unusual occurrences, and signs of danger. On a small boat such as Fred's, one person usually is enough to ensure safety. The larger and more complex the vessel, though, the more hands are needed, reminding us that "navigation" is not just about charts and coordinates, but also about execution and teamwork. This teamwork applies to launching, sailing, and docking. The more people you have working, the better off you will be, and the safer, more productive the journey.

It is the same in the body of Christ. When everyone is doing his or her SOMEthing, then there are more "hands on deck" helping to navigate the church and to make sure that our efforts are productive and that we are sailing in safe, workable waters.

Have you ever heard of the 80/20 rule? This rule, which permeates just about every church family I know, says that 20 percent of the people do 80 percent of the work. I have a couple of theories for why this might be the case.

First, most people do not know their spiritual gifts. They don't know how to serve, but, many times, they have not been shown the importance of everyone working together. Add to this that some folks are just lazy and don't really want to broaden their horizons, people for whom church is a one-day-a-week task that they "check off" each Sunday morning, and you get the picture.

Second, I think some churches experience the 80/20 rule because we let them, and because, as my friend likes to say, there is very little "skin in the game" for most Christians. What he means by this is that, many times, church doesn't really require much from people. If they get unhappy, they either force out the leadership or they leave and choose another church.

On the water, everyone is in the same boat, literally, and if the waters get rough, there is no going overboard. Everyone learns to play his or her part, and quickly they get some "skin in the game."

One of the best things that could happen to the church is for us to make church more important, more critical to our daily lives, like a vessel on the open waters. It should matter, not because our parents or someone in authority said it matters, but because we have bought into the mission and significance of what God is doing. The church, with "all hands on deck" doing what God has gifted them to do, can navigate any difficulty and lead to great accomplishments.

First Conflicts

It has always amazed and somewhat amused me that the first conflict in the early church was not about theology or doctrinal issues. It was about who would make sure that the widows and those less fortunate would be fed and served appropriately (see Acts 6). Of course, one group in the early church felt its members were receiving less care than the others. So the apostles set up a committee (maybe they did not call it such, but it was a committee nonetheless!) to make sure that no one was being left out. True to form, the first church conflict was not about doctrine and not about theological discourse but about a program in need of better organization.

My first church conflict was similar. When I arrived at the church, no one instructed me on all of the "special things" that the pastor was supposed to do in the community. Many just assumed that I would know. I didn't, of course, and within just a few weeks I was facing my first conflict because a certain ladies' Bible study was not being cared for as they had so long expected. When I mentioned that someone else might be able to lead their group better, they were aghast that I would suggest such a thing. The pastor had *always* done that. With the "old" pastors no longer there, church members had no real idea about all that these pastors had done, except in the context of their own little piece of the pie. When the new pastor didn't show up to "garnish" that piece, the pie grew very bitter.

I learned quickly that I could not do everything that they expected. The average tenure of the pastors before me had dropped to only two years. There was a terrible burnout rate, and I didn't want to follow suit. Our answer was to deploy members according to their spiritual gifts and to utilize folks in those areas where they could serve best and be most effective.

The by-product was not only that more people became involved, working in areas where they felt called and were excited to serve, but fewer things fell through the cracks, because someone was always connected, someone always had ownership and made sure that if their particular area was in need, the appropriate people would be notified.

Paul writes in 1 Corinthians 12:27, "Now you are the body of Christ and individually members of it." Several parts of this short verse became critically important to my understanding (and thus to my leadership) in that first church appointment. First, Paul says that "all of you *together* are Christ's body" (emphasis added). Not *part* of you or *one* of you or *the leader* of you, but "all of you" are Christ's body. There is no separating what God's intentions are for setting up the system in this way. When the body of Christ works together in doing our SOMEthings, we become the living, breathing expression of Christ—we become no less than Christ's body.

Second, Paul reminds us that we all have a special gift and that we are separately to discover, deepen, and deploy it in the work of the Body. Don't forget, Paul encourages that we are *necessary*. That means each of us and all of us—even you. Without you and your gift and your SOMEthing that God has planted in your life, we cannot fully navigate the difficult waters. Sure, the Adversary is always working to trip us up. He likes nothing more than for us to feel alone, divided, and useless on the large ocean by ourselves. He doesn't have to destroy us, just distract us enough that we miss the power of what God is doing in our midst, and thus we lose our way. When the body of Christ is acting like . . . well . . . Christ, together we are the most potent force on the planet. The Adversary knows this. *We* should not only know it, but live like it, too.

CHAPTER 13
We Are *Yoked* Together

Matthew 5:13-16

Our Friends Under the Bridge

"Do they belong to us?" It sounds like an odd question, but not to a three-year-old trying to make sense of why the folks living under the bridge have nowhere to go. My youngest daughter, Emma Leigh, and I had taken a day trip to New Orleans, some eighty-five miles from where we were living at the time. It was a couple of years after Hurricane Katrina had ravaged the city, and although many volunteer service groups have made life a little more bearable for the masses of homeless people who live in New Orleans, the underpasses of Interstate 10 were still filled with those who had no other place to go. One part, in particular, is filled with those living in such conditions. This is the Canal Street exit. As soon as you turn off of the interstate, you stop at a traffic light. On either side, behind you, and in front of you are people living in cardboard boxes, under blankets and, some, out in the elements—all living in a makeshift city "under" the underpass.

I had noticed the scene before, but, on that day, I was surprised by the number. Emma Leigh saw them too. She was three years old at the time, and although she was still a baby in so many ways, she had the vocabulary of a child much older, largely due to her having older sisters who included and involved Emma Leigh in almost every make-believe world they created. As she and I drove along, I adjusted my rearview mirror to watch her eyes. That is when she asked, "Daddy, who are they?" I explained that the men and women under the bridge didn't have homes, and that they were living the best way they knew. It was then that Emma Leigh stunned me: "Why don't their mommies and daddies come get them?" she asked. In her little world, everyone had mommies and daddies who took care of their children. I wondered how many of the people we were seeing now had wished the same thing.

I explained to Emma Leigh that many of them no longer had a family or that they couldn't get in touch with their family, or that for some of them, their family members were mad at them or they were mad at their families. I could tell in her eyes that this did not make sense. All she knew was a family who loved her very much, and who would go anywhere to take care of her and to make sure that she was okay. In fact, only a few weeks prior to that trip, she had called me at the office and had been tired and upset. "Can you come get me, Daddy?" she asked. "Of course I can," I replied. When she needed her daddy, he showed up. That is what daddies and mommies and families do. In fact, she had a whole host of folks who would respond. If for some reason she couldn't have gotten me, she would have certainly contacted her grandmothers or her aunt.

To have *no one*; this did not compute for Emma Leigh, and I could tell that she did not know what to do with this idea. After a few beats, she replied, "That's okay. They can go live with their friends." Once again, in Emma Leigh's world, friends took care of each other. Then, as though she was ready for what my answer might be to that, she added, ". . . or call their church." Now it was getting personal and painful, and I knew that at some point, this three-year-old would make too much sense even for this situation.

Again, I tried to explain that their situations were difficult, and that they might not have friends who could or would help. That didn't seem to sit well with Emma Leigh either. She sat there for a second while I kept wondering why the traffic light was taking so long to change. Finally, feeling the need to say something, I blurted out, "They just don't belong to anyone, sweetheart."

It was at that moment that my three-year-old daughter got the best of me. Jesus' instructions to his disciples that they should approach the Father as a child meant something in that moment, and I, for one, confronted it firsthand.

"Don't they belong to *us*, Daddy?" she finally responded. This was my three-year-old daughter's way of asking, *Aren't we their friends?* She didn't say anything else; she didn't need to. Her point hit home and reminded me that what unites us is so much deeper than what we allow to divide us—*allow* being the key word.

My three-year-old reminded me that all of us are yoked together by the sheer essence of being the children of God. It didn't matter what our skin color was, where we were born, how much we had attended church, or how much we knew about our Bibles. We are all yoked together, first by the fact that we are all God's children; and second, by the fact that God's children don't get to pick their brothers and sisters.

You Matter

My best friend is one of the most spiritual people I know. Everything about his life is framed within the context of Scripture. His three-pronged approach to the faith goes like this: pray, read your Bible, and love Jesus. Whenever his children would go out at night, once they had gotten old enough to drive, he always told them to "be salt and light." His words came from Matthew 5:13-16, where Jesus tells those gathered at the Sermon on the Mount that they are "the salt of the earth" and "the light of the world." This was Jesus' benediction to the Beatitudes, a discussion of what many believe to be the values of Jesus.

When I founded the church that I would pastor for nearly ten years, I started closing the services with the phrase "Be salt and light." It was a nice way to finish the service and to remind people of the importance of living faithfully for God every day. So much of what Jesus said in those words of the Sermon on the Mount was about the ways that we are united by God's love for us and our love of God. Jesus reminded the listeners that when we live the way God has intended, not only are we important to God's plan, but we matter as to how God's love is shared and experienced in the world. When we act and live as God's children, we are yoked together by more than common interests—we are joined together by a common heritage as the heirs of the Kingdom. That is why the Apostle Paul says that we belong no longer to ourselves but wholly and completely to Christ. And, if we belong to Christ, we ultimately belong to each other.

A Most Troubling Delivery

My mother's father was a difficult, troubled man. He had been a hemophiliac back in a day when there was little to treat the disease except for outdated pain medications and odd concoctions called "horse serum." My grandfather, whose name was Randolph, also had an angry heart and, at times, a violent spirit. He was known to beat my grandmother and her children, including my mother. He was small in stature but not afraid of a fight (even with his condition) and could come off as mean and arrogant. He was also very bright and used his intellect to hold sway over many people.

Adding to the drama was the fact that Randolph was a very nice-looking man and very popular with women. In fact, as my grandmother would learn later, he had numerous girlfriends throughout the county.

One particular girlfriend really had his attention, and, later, it was believed that her two children were actually Randolph's and not her husband's. This was a "different time," others would say, and mostly, people looked the other way. Their real regret was for my grandmother, who was a wonderful, beautiful woman on the inside and out, and who, throughout the years, in spite of his terrible treatment of her, sought to please Randolph but could not find a way to ease his restless, cruel spirit.

Still people remained silent and let things go. Until . . .

Randolph, on more than one occasion, had warned my grandmother, whose name was Dorothy, that she was to spend no money on anything. Although Randolph made good money as a surveyor, planter, and timber salesman, he kept most of the money for himself. Dorothy, though, had a dream of being a teacher and had wanted to learn to drive and buy a car so that she could attend the local college to take classes and get her degree. Randolph would hear nothing of it, saying that he had no extra funds to assist her.

However, one day the local car dealership in town delivered a brand-new car to the front door of Dorothy's home. She ran out, screaming with excitement. On top of the car was a large red bow, a gift from Randolph. As Dorothy walked around the car looking over the beautiful blue color and the new, spotless upholstery, Randolph drove up. He got out and ordered Dorothy out of the car, and then he dragged the car dealer, who had driven the car there, by one arm to talk at a nearby tree. Randolph shook his finger and in as low a voice as possible gave the car dealer the talk of his life. Eventually the dealer came back to the car, got inside, and drove away. Later it was learned that the dealer had delivered Randolph's gift to the wrong woman. The car was not for his wife, but for his mistress.

After several days, word spread throughout the community about what had happened. People were outraged. Most of them knew of Randolph's ways, of his mistresses, and of the way he treated Dorothy. They knew that Dorothy would give anything simply to have a way to go to town, to the market, and to school, to have some freedom and to make a life for herself apart from this vicious man.

After hearing of this episode, a distant cousin of Dorothy's down the road finally had enough and decided to take up money—coins, dollars, big and little donations alike—to buy Dorothy a car. Not only did he raise enough money to buy a decent used car, but he helped Dorothy enroll in school, and then when time came for her to attend her first class, this cousin and his wife babysat Dorothy's children.

As was to be expected, Randolph was furious and eventually landed on the porch of the cousin, calling him out of his house. What Randolph did not realize was that his ranting and raving had aroused the suspicion of the neighbors. One neighbor called another. That neighbor called another neighbor, who called another. Finally, within a matter of ten minutes, about ten families had walked across their fields and were standing around the gentleman who had helped my grandmother. By the end of the conversation, with these neighbors no longer simply standing by and watching what Randolph had done so freely, not only was Randolph told that he would not prevent Dorothy from going to school, but he was also told that he would have to provide for her tuition. If he didn't, he was told, then he, himself, would pay the consequences, one neighbor at a time.

Finally, realizing that he was outnumbered, Randolph backed down off of the porch, got into his car, and went home. He never hit Dorothy or his children again. He allowed her to go to school, and eventually she graduated with a degree in teaching.

About a year later, Randolph died under suspicious circumstances. It was believed that he was killed by the brothers of a woman in another county with whom he had been involved. Regardless, few missed him, knowing that no matter how difficult her life would be, Dorothy had a chance to do more than survive and that she would prosper. This same community of people helped her finish her degree, and eventually she paid them back by teaching most of their children and grandchildren and great-grandchildren over the next thirty-five years.

It was a difficult scene in my family's history, but it is a story that we all believed must be told, because it testifies to the best of who and what we are together. My grandmother's neighbors decided to do SOMEthing; and when they did, they yoked themselves together with a beaten-down young woman and changed her life. Because she made something of herself, she would go on to change the lives of many others, including my mother and me.

God could have made this complex, but God didn't. God could have made the requirements so high that none of us could reach them, but God didn't. God could have worked the dynamics so that only those who held certain religious or spiritual qualifications could make a difference in the world. But—you guessed it—God didn't do that either. God made it simple. When Christians work together for the right things in the right ways in the right seasons for the right cause, ANYthing is possible. It is God's plan . . . to change a community or even just one life at a time.

Friend, the plan is in place, the encouragement is present, and the time is now. Your SOMEthing must be done. What do you say? Better yet, where shall we begin?

Loving Jesus . . . Loving Like Jesus

An Unexpected Verdict

Dan was a successful attorney, but he was not as successful at life. He arrived at my office on a Monday and proceeded to ask for "the best advice" I could give him about "why faith should matter." He wanted an answer immediately. However, I asked him to give me a few days, and I spent several days thinking about what I should share.

The night before our next meeting I awoke and wrote two phrases on the pad sitting on the nightstand. They were "Love Jesus" and "Love like Jesus." I couldn't think of anything more important for those of us who call ourselves Christian. Certainly, it is not enough that we know Jesus and that we say we want to live like him. Instead, we put our energies into loving him, knowing him, understanding him, becoming like him. Then we live our energies, loving like he did those who are the most forgotten and considered to be "the least of these" among our brothers and sisters.

After sharing these phrases with my friend, I watched as his life changed. This change was not the result of my words or wisdom, but the simplicity of God working in him to transform his priorities and his life. He began to read his Bible more, and he attended one Bible study and one life-study class after another. He became a regular in the church, and he volunteered to serve in many different serving opportunities. He also joined a small accountability group that provided a new approach to community. Dan searched for something more, something deeper. He knew he needed to begin by loving Jesus more, but his real goal was not to "know more" but to "live differently." And he did.

But, even with all of this, it was not enough for Dan. After several months, Dan resigned from his law firm to take the directorship of a community ministry association that ministers to the needs of the under-resourced. It was a huge life decision, but one that provided a new joy and direction for his life. Of course, it shocked everyone who had known "the old Dan"; but those of us who had watched his life over the past months knew that he wanted more from the journey.

Over the next few years, Dan's life flourished and his work made a difference. Dan not only did amazing things in helping those in need, but he changed the spirit of his own life. Maybe most important, he changed the spirit of his family, his friends, his small group, and his church. People could not help noticing what had happened in his life. They saw the changes where Dan seemed more at peace, more content; and they also saw the joy and presence of mind that gave his life purpose. But, as significant as this was, it was nothing compared to the results of what God was doing through Dan's newfound career and motives. The more he gave his life away in service to others, the more he found the real meaning of his life. Before, Dan's life had been successful; now, it was *significant*.

How About You?

So, what about *your* life? Are you happy with the status quo, with getting by with the same old routines that lead to lots of activity but few results? Have you felt the pressure to be everything to everyone, but you end up feeling as though you are nothing—or, at least, very little—to anyone? When you do find something that gives you joy, excitement, and a feeling of purpose, how does that translate into what God really needs for you to accomplish, both for yourself and also within the body of Christ?

The questions keep coming, because this is about more than getting our calendars in order, getting our "to-do" lists straight, or deciding what our next volunteer ministry will be. This is how we are wired up. This is the way God has framed our being. Apart from experiencing God's presence, this—all that we have talked about in this book and especially in these last pages—*this is what relationship in Christ is all about*. It is the lynchpin of the good news, that Christ has transformed our lives and wants us to live as that transformed presence in the world.

My friend, this is not supposed to be complicated. You have much to offer in the body of Christ. God has gifted you—yes, you—and I want to help you discover that area of passion and the way God has wired you up to accomplish significant things for the Kingdom. Sure, in the larger frame, this is part of the gospel imperative, but it is also part of your birthright as a child of God.

Faith in Christ is more than signing your name in the attendance books on Sunday morning or volunteering at some ministry or program in your church (though those are both very important). No, it is about awakening the very image of God inside of you and then sharing that with the world. And (and this is a big "And") as you are doing that in your life, others are doing the same thing, and the body of Christ awakens together to accomplish something significant.

Someone once asked a small, aging nun in one of the most economically depressed parts of the world why it was that even with her failing health, she marched into the courtyard of the convent every morning to care for the countless sick and dying people who lay on the makeshift stretchers. After all, the person said, she was far too aged for this heavy burden and work, and had, certainly, paid her dues. After a moment, this wonderful woman of God (not unlike any of us in her love, doubts, fears, and joys for Jesus) looked up and said, "Because this is how they will see Christ . . . and how I will see him, too." Simple. Powerful. Enough.

The convent in question was in Calcutta, India. The patients were AIDS victims, people with leprosy, and people dying of diseases with no names yet. The woman was Mother Teresa. She couldn't do EVERYthing. . . . So she did SOMEthing. The rest is history.

Go make history, my friend. The world needs you, your gift, your SOMEthing . . . now.

Discussion and Reflection Guide

Loving Jesus . . . Loving Like Jesus

The following guide provides two parts for a week of intensive study and reflection for loving Jesus . . . and loving like Jesus in the world. As we have discussed, it is not enough that we love God or know God's principles. Certainly, it is important. Going deeper in our relationship with Christ, however, is about more than memorizing verses and knowing the right doctrine. It is about building a significant, consuming, devoted relationship that then propels us into the world as the "hands and feet of Jesus." Then we are able to use what we know about faith in Christ to change our communities, affect the lives of those we love and those God sends into our paths, and meet the various challenges of a world in such need of distinct change and difference.

The first part is a "Daily Challenge," used as a way of knowing God's word more and for spending quality time with the Creator each day. The Daily Challenge also encourages community/fellowship, prayer, and acts of kindness as sacred connections to God and others. The Daily Challenge is based on the "first devotions" of those believers in Acts 2:42.

The guide then unveils seven themes that allow for us to know Christ more and to go deeper in our devotion to Christ and our affection for God's people. At the end of each day, you will also find suggestions for discovering your spiritual gifts (though that is also the main focus of Day Four). You will also learn to take your spiritual gifts (your SOMEthing) and use them passionately to affect change in the world and make a difference.

The model for this, as we have mentioned, is Acts 2:42-47 and the story of the first-century church. By studying these first Christians, we recognize their devotion to Christ, watch the deepening of their relationships, and then witness the unfolding of their community into a living, breathing expression of Christ in action. The results are palpable. They are affected in a variety of ways, not the least of which is the way they view and treat one another and the world.

Is that not what this book or any book about the good news should reveal? That loving Jesus is a profound "shakeup" of the way the world does things and that, having been impacted by its grace, we are no longer the same?

So I hope you enjoy this study and reflection time as an opportunity to know this Jesus who has loved you so, and then to crave, yes, crave, that you might live like him in our world.

The Daily Challenge

We begin with suggestions for use every day in our personal devotional life. This challenge provides a framework for how we then encounter these principles and for how we live out our spiritual gifts.

- Read your Bible for eight minutes a day. Write down your thoughts about what you read.
- Make contact with an old friend, a new friend, a family member, and a person with whom your relationship may be strained. Live out "fellowship."
- Do one act of random kindness and service this week. Live as the "hands and feet of Jesus."
- Pray daily and make a list of your requests and God's responses.

Day One: Studying God's Word

Scripture Focus

Read Jeremiah 9:23-24.

Questions

1. Would God be pleased with the state of your heart or with your current level of understanding of God's word?
2. Start a study journal of your daily challenges. What verses is God showing you as important to your relationship with God?
3. What does God consider as the most important part of being in relationship?
4. What does it mean to "understand and know" God?

Life Lesson and Focus

Learning to love Jesus through deeper connections with God through God's word. How does knowing God's word have a deeper impact on the way God is forming you to serve and witness in the world?

Day Two: Doing Life Together with Your Brothers and Sisters

Scripture Focus

Read John 13:34-35.

Questions

1. Are you ready to shatter the masks we live behind and learn to live in biblical community with our brothers and sisters in the faith?
2. What does it mean to "love one another" the way "Christ has loved us"?

3. Why is it important that the world "recognize" that we are disciples of Christ?

Life Lesson and Focus

Learning to love Jesus through deeper connections in small groups and in fellowship with God's people. How does this lesson impact the way we live our faith in the world? How does "knowing others" and being "known by others" shape our spiritual witness and relationships in Christ?

Day Three: Learning to Share Our Resources

Scripture Focus

Read Proverbs 3:9.

Questions

1. Do we practice healthy financial values that allow for us to work faithfully, save appropriately, and give generously in service to Christ's work and his church?
2. What does it mean to "honor God with everything"? And what does the "first and the best" represent in your giving habits for God?
3. How does the way we spend our money reflect what we consider to be important in our relationship with Christ?
4. What can we do to reshape our financial values to be more generous and to provide a stronger witness for Christ?

Life Lesson and Focus

Learning to love Jesus through tithing and through sacrificial giving. Are we tithing? If not, how can we work into a tithing relationship with Christ? If so, is God calling us to sacrificial giving?

Day Four: Discovering Our Spiritual Gifts

Scripture Focus

Read 1 Corinthians 12:1-14.

Questions

1. Why is it important for us to know our spiritual gifts?
2. If God has given everyone a spiritual gift, how does our knowledge and implementation of that gift affect the plan of God for our community? What are some of the different kinds of gifts?
3. Why did God include these gifts as important to God's plan?
4. So, everyone has a gift, and every gift is important. What can you do today in order to discover and then use your spiritual gift?

Life Lesson and Focus

Learning to love Jesus through discovering and implementing our spiritual gifts. Sign up for a spiritual gift discernment class at your local church. Spend time understanding the different spiritual gifts and why they are important to the entire body of Christ. How do your gifts increase or challenge the work of God around you and in your church?

Day Five: Serving Faithfully and Selflessly Utilizing Your Spiritual Gifts

Scripture Focus

Read Matthew 5:13-16.

Questions

1. Do you serve in an extended capacity beyond regular worship attendance giving back to those in need, to the life of the

church, or to the global concerns of individuals and communities around the world?

2. Why do you believe God considers serving beyond our own comfort zones critical for us to know God more?
3. What ways can you serve today and be involved in making a difference in your community and the world?
4. How has discovering your spiritual gifts informed your areas of service in the body of Christ and in the world?

Life Lesson and Focus

Learning to love Jesus through a serving lifestyle. Develop a lifestyle of serving and for responding to the needs of others. Make a list of needs and volunteer opportunities in your church or community that you can easily volunteer for during the next week. If you don't volunteer, write God a letter as to why you couldn't find the time.

Day Six: Living the Disciplines

Scripture Focus

Read 1 Corinthians 1:18-29.

Questions

1. The spiritual disciplines were established as markers to remind and guide us as we draw close to God. They also give us glimpses into what God is working on and doing in our lives. What does it mean for us to "live the disciplines" of the faith?
2. What do the disiplines teach you about God's work in your life?
3. What does it mean for us to "boast in Christ" and not in ourselves?
4. Why did God choose the "lowly" and "least" in order to teach the most important lessons?

Life Lesson and Focus

Learning to love Jesus by living the disciplines. The spiritual disciplines are a means by which we find different routes and angles for recognizing God's plan in our lives. To discover our SOMEthing might require prayer, fasting, journaling, and serving in order to see the full measure of God's love for us.

Day Seven: Celebrative Worship

We love Jesus "by celebrative worship that points our attention and the attention of others back to God."

Scripture Focus

Read Psalm 138:1-5.

Questions

1. Have we given back our whole hearts and complete lives in worship?
2. Do we celebrate and understand the true nature of worship as a means of "pointing back to God" and providing a doorway for building relationship both with Christ and with God's people?
3. How does knowing what God has done in our lives impact the depth and power of our worship?
4. What does it mean for God to step into our spiritual lives and proclaim his greatness and wonder into our hearts?

Life Lesson and Focus

Learning to love Jesus through celebrative worship in varying styles and forms. When was the last time you wrote God a "thank-you letter" for all that God has done for your life? What about a worship journal, listing the ways that God is working in your life and the ways you "worship" God daily, not just on Sunday?

APPENDIX
Understanding and Identifying Spiritual Gifts

God shares spiritual gifts with us to accomplish God's work and provide for a more complete, whole approach to living out the work of God faithfully in the world. To that end, there are several biblical "truths" associated with spiritual gifts:

1. God established the various spiritual gifts for implementation of the gospel imperative to accomplish significant advancement for the Kingdom.
2. Each person has been given at least one primary spiritual passion area that lines up with his or her "spiritual DNA."
3. Each person has been given at least one primary spiritual gift for living as the "hands and feet of Jesus" in the world.
4. Each person has been "wired" up with a distinctive personality and temperament that frame the work of the spiritual gift within the person's passion area.
5. God is faithful to bless the implementation of the spiritual gift, with prayer and discernment for strength and guidance of the body of Christ, with the passion area in order to maintain the work of the gospel and sharing of the good news.
6. God is also faithful to raise up those who will implement a particular spiritual gift within a passion area in the case that the person whose gift is identified does not "step up" for service.
7. At the end of the day, spiritual gifts in the service of the faithful are the means by which the body of Christ will live out the dynamics of God's will.

Discovering Your Spiritual Gift

1. Pray for God's guidance in identifying those passion areas where God has preconditioned your heart for service and where, through grace, God has given you a "Kingdom Vision." In other words, what "keeps you up at night" or "becomes your nonnegotiable" Kingdom focus?

2. Use the Scriptures to identify those gifts most matching your spiritual DNA. Making a list of those attributes, in the definitions, practically, and within Scripture, is helpful for narrowing those gifts most suited to your makeup and patterns of spiritual practice.

3. Take a spiritual gifts class and use a spiritual gift inventory to narrow the focus of those gifts most related to your area of passion.

4. Allow for your covenant group, response team, or spiritual mentor to verify and validate the spiritual gift assessment.

5. Take a spiritual gifts class and use a personal temperament and personality guide to develop your personal style for implementation of the spiritual gift assessment.